FINDING FORM WITH FIBRE

be inspired
gather materials
create your own sculptural basketry

Ruth Woods

In memory of my brother Geoff Woods who inspired me on my creative journey from a very young age.

Copyright 2022 © Ruth Woods

All rights reserved. No part of this publication may be reproduced or transmitted by any means, electronic, photocopying or otherwise without permission of the Author.

All artwork featured in this book is the copyright of the artists.

ISBN 978-0-6484858-1-0

All illustrations by Ruth Woods

Graphic Design by Michelle Lorimer
Email: hello@michellelorimer.com

Main Photographers
Ben Willis
Sean Paris
Ruth Woods

Printed by IngramSpark
Printed in Australia
First Edition 2022

Published by Ruth Woods
Healesville, Victoria 3777
Australia

www.craftschooloz.com

We would like to acknowledge the Wurundjeri people as the Traditional Custodians of the land that we call home. We pay our respects to their Elders, past and present, and respect their continuing culture and customs, wisdom, and teachings of Country that have nurtured this land for so long.

We also acknowledge and pay respect to all First Nations people as the Traditional Custodians of this continent, whose cultures are among the oldest living cultures in human history.

Photo of Mt. Riddell by Sean Paris

FOREWORD

by Lisa Cahill

CEO and Artistic Director
Australian Design Centre

Basketry is an ancient craft. It is perhaps our earliest example of sustainable craft practice using bio-degradable materials. From Aboriginal and Torres Strait Islander people weaving grasses and reeds for functional use, to contemporary forms with new materials and techniques, basketry remains a distinctive and important practice today.

Ruth Woods in her book *Finding Form with Fibre* profiles the work of 14 artists working today. These artists are producing new and conceptually thoughtful work across an exciting diversity of sculptural practice. Many are focussed on how to make their practice sustainable by using plant-based and recycled materials. These makers are resourceful and thoughtful about ensuring their creative practice is environmentally conscious while at the same time seeking to draw our attention to the beauty and fragility of the natural world. Sculptural basketry is also a socio-cultural practice with many of the makers drawing on their richly diverse cultural traditions and backgrounds to develop a their own unique contemporary practice.

Joy and a sense of accomplishment comes from exploring our creativity. A creative practice can have enormous benefits for our mental health and wellbeing. This book is a fantastic guide to practice: a starting point for new makers; a reference for established makers; and a pleasure to read for anyone interested in woven forms. The pages are filled with resources and ideas for the how to weave and the immense variety of materials to use.

A characteristic of craft is that makers with mastery pass on skills and techniques to new makers. It is in that spirit of generosity that Ruth Woods, an educator and an artist, has crafted this book so that basketry may continue to thrive inspiring new generations of craftspeople.

CONTENTS

6   INTRODUCTION

8   ARTISTS — *A collection of fourteen Australian Fibre Basketry Artists working with a variety of plant-based and recycled materials.*

66   MATERIALS — *Information on useful plants and other recommended new and recycled materials, that can be incorporated into sculptural basketry work.*

114   CREATE — *Instructions for key basketry techniques to develop Practice Projects, developing ideas and moving on to sculptural forms.*

176   ABOUT THE AUTHOR
179   CRAFT SCHOOL OZ
180   BIBLIOGRAPHY
181   ACKNOWLEDGEMENTS
182   RESOURCES
184   FIND ARTISTS & CONTRIBUTORS
186   INDEX

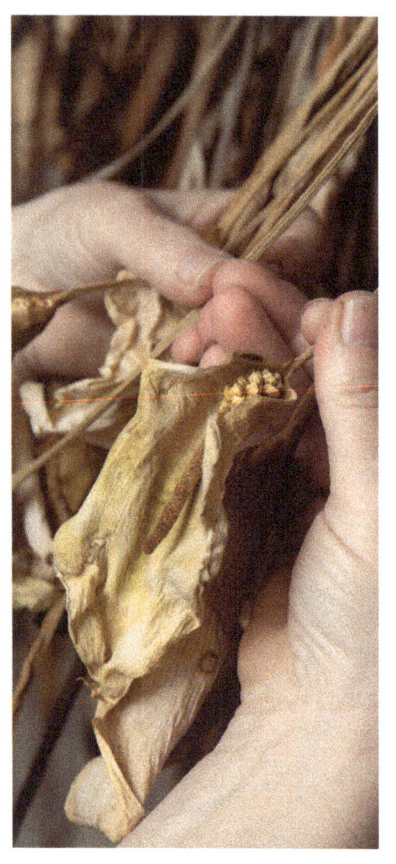

INTRODUCTION

The seed for this book has gradually grown out of my years teaching basketry and textile crafts around Australia. At the end of a class, it was common for people to ask for other resources that would help them discover techniques using plant fibres and other materials; few publications would come to mind.

While on my travels I was privileged to meet many inspiring fibre and basketry artists using both plant fibre and recycled materials. Creating this book was an opportunity to celebrate these creators and assist in showcasing their work.

This book captures a broad repository of knowledge in a way that shows the beauty of these artists' work and teaches techniques in a way that is simple to follow and inspire.

An important part of my creative practice is that where possible, I use materials that are readily available and sustainable - so plant fibre fits beautifully into this scope and there so many plants to choose from. However I see more and more artists using recycled materials, making environmental statements and creating some intriguing artwork.

A few years after I started teaching, I watched an ABC Australia 'War on Waste' documentary and was stunned to learn that across the continent, we add 6000 kg of textile waste to landfill every ten minutes.

This sobering fact made my practice seem more important than ever, so while focussing on teaching and using plant fibre and recycled materials, the environmental message was also very important.

How to use this book

Browse through the Artists section of the book and enjoy works by an impressive group of creators. You cannot help but be inspired.

Start to collect the materials that you have access to; there are many suggestions in the Materials section with a comprehensive list of plants and other fibres.

Create 'Practice Projects' and explore techniques. A Practice Project is a way to play and experiment with no outcome in mind. You can simply trial a few methods and play with what you have. Try not to judge what you make, embrace those imperfections - just keep exploring. Enjoying yourself while you're creating is so important. It's not only good for your development as a creative person but beneficial for your well-being.

Allow yourself to get into a creative space and allocate yourself time. The flow of making and being in that creative space enables you to acquire new skills and techniques as demonstrated in this book.

Lastly, do not forget to use an old-fashioned notebook to capture your ideas before they are lost. You will be surprised what happens when you have a visual record of creative thoughts - it's where ideas flow and magic is made.

ARTISTS

The artists featured in this book have used an array of materials for their work; from plant fibre, recycled plastic, wire and even ocean rope. They are authentic makers exploring their mediums to push the boundaries of basketry sculpture taken from a traditional craft to contemporary expression.

Their influences range from nature, the environment, social commentary and a rich cultural heritage.

Techniques used have been broad and varied, working and experimenting with an array of different fibres.

They come from many different backgrounds - academic, medical and crafting, some for many years. They also include Australian Indigenous women with a strong cultural lineage who share their story with traditional fibres and techniques.

We are privileged to be allowed into their lives through their work, where they share their ideas and influences, their materials of choice and their own unique connection to their craft.

ANNE JILLETT
Page 10

KYLIE CALDWELL
Page 38

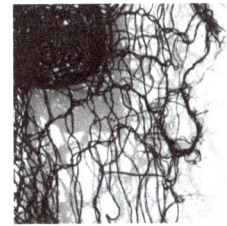
BROOKE MUNRO
Page 14

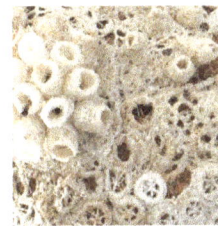
MARION GAEMERS
Page 42

DELISSA WALKER
Page 18

MAVIS GANAMBARR
Page 46

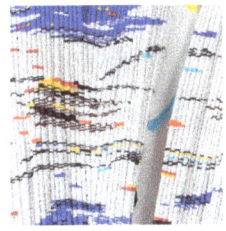
FLEUR BRETT
Page 22

NICOLE ROBINS
Page 50

HELLE JORGENSEN
Page 26

PAULA DO PRADO
Page 54

JESS LEITMANIS
Page 30

SALLY BLAKE
Page 58

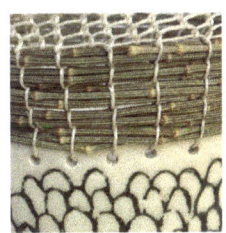
JUSTINE WELLMAN
Page 34

ZORA VERONA
Page 62

ANNE JILLETT

This page:
Ocean Relics - detail
Photo by the artist
Fibres: Lomandra, acrylic yarn & driftwood

Opposite page:
Ocean Relics - detail
Photo by the artist
Fibres: Lomandra, acrylic yarn & driftwood

Anne Jillett's creative sanctuary lies in the foothills of Mt Bellenden Ker in Far North Queensland. It's a corner of the earth no stranger to tropical downpours, or the lush rainforests that it propagates. Anne's art studio overlooks a rich expanse of ancient canopies dating back to the time of Gondwana. Wooroonooran (translates to 'black rock') National Park is Anne's local park, a part of the heritage listed tropical forest that stretches as far as Cooktown to the north, and Townsville to the south. It's a jaw-dropping landscape that provides a corridor for the endangered cassowary and other species that have been able to flourish within this wet environmental time warp. And, like many of her contemporaries, Anne attributes her natural surroundings as being an integral source of inspiration.

Anne has always felt a special affinity with the ocean; particularly the crystal blue waters of Far North Queensland. It is here that she finds stones, shells and driftwood to incorporate into her work – each piece of debris shaped by its own unique ocean voyage. Anne is passionate about the preservation of this natural environment, but is quick to point out that she is not an activist. "It's not my intention to preach through art, although I do hope that by creating objects that resonate with the natural world, people are reminded what a vital life source it is."

Growing up, Anne learnt to knit as soon as her hands had ample dexterity. She could sew her own clothes from the age of ten, developing a love of the handmade and upcycling from recycled fabrics. "I love the originality of handmade objects and the tactile nature of textiles," she explains. These days she enjoys making cordage from preloved clothing and uses sewing scraps to make functional and sculptural forms.

As a student in the 1970s, Anne found herself encouraged to enrol in a law degree. Her parents weren't enthusiastic about their daughter's ambitions to become an artist, she explains dryly. "Salvation," she says, "came in the form of a full scholarship to study art teaching." During her studies she found that sculpture piqued her interest more than anything else. Anne's career in education took her to the Torres Straits for several years where she absorbed the Aboriginal and Torres Strait cultures and artworks.

Anne's insight into the world of basketry came through weaving workshops. The first, with Lena Yarinkura from Maningrida in Arnhem Land, who taught her how to twine and make coil baskets from pandanus leaves. The second, with Rhonda Brim from Kuranda, who taught her how to make dilly bags, an indigenous Australian bag usually made from Lomandra in the wet tropics. Rhonda's introduction of this native grass as a basketry material would have a profound impact on the development of Anne's own distinct style of basketry.

It was a chance meeting in 2010 that was to change the course of Anne's artistic practice. At a time when Anne felt burnt out from the demands of a stressful job, she met Mary-Anne Tokome Amu at her stall in the iconic Rusty's Markets Cairns. Mary-Anne was selling beautiful Papua New Guinean bilums, bags that are traditionally woven by women from thigh spun string using a figure eight loop. (Mary-Anne is from

Wapenamanda in the Enga Provence of the Papua New Guinean highlands). After chatting, Mary-Anne offered to teach Anne how to make her own. Of their classes, Anne explains, "Each Saturday, I would sit on a milk crate next to her, learning this wonderful craft. We shared life stories, learned about each other's cultures, and laughed a lot."

Through Mary-Anne, Anne met other Papua women who generously taught her the finer points of bilum making and the intricate pattern work that came with it. "I learned that Papua New Guinean's prefer bilums made from acrylic knitting yarn, for its strength and washability – and the variety of colours available. These colours can lead to incredibly striking pattern work." New patterns, she explains, evolve all the time.

Today, Anne chooses a hybrid mix of acrylic and natural materials. For its robustness and strength,

she will use stripped Lomandra for a basket's core, and then acrylic knitting yarn thigh spun into string. The process, she explains, allows for a mix of colour, and a distinctness in her own unique style. For Anne, the evolution of each piece is never obvious from the start. She enters each work with an open mind, and although labour intensive, finds the process of making to be meditative. Each piece, she says, provides a vehicle for mindfulness, gifting her with the mental space to think and be open to new creative ideas. She likes to see her work as, 'Like a leap of faith, both scary and exciting'.

Much like life itself, really.

This page:
Ocean's Gift
Photo by the artist
Fibres: Lomandra, acrylic yarn & driftwood

Opposite page:
Ocean Relics
Photo by the artist
Fibres: Lomandra, acrylic yarn & driftwood

BROOKE MUNRO

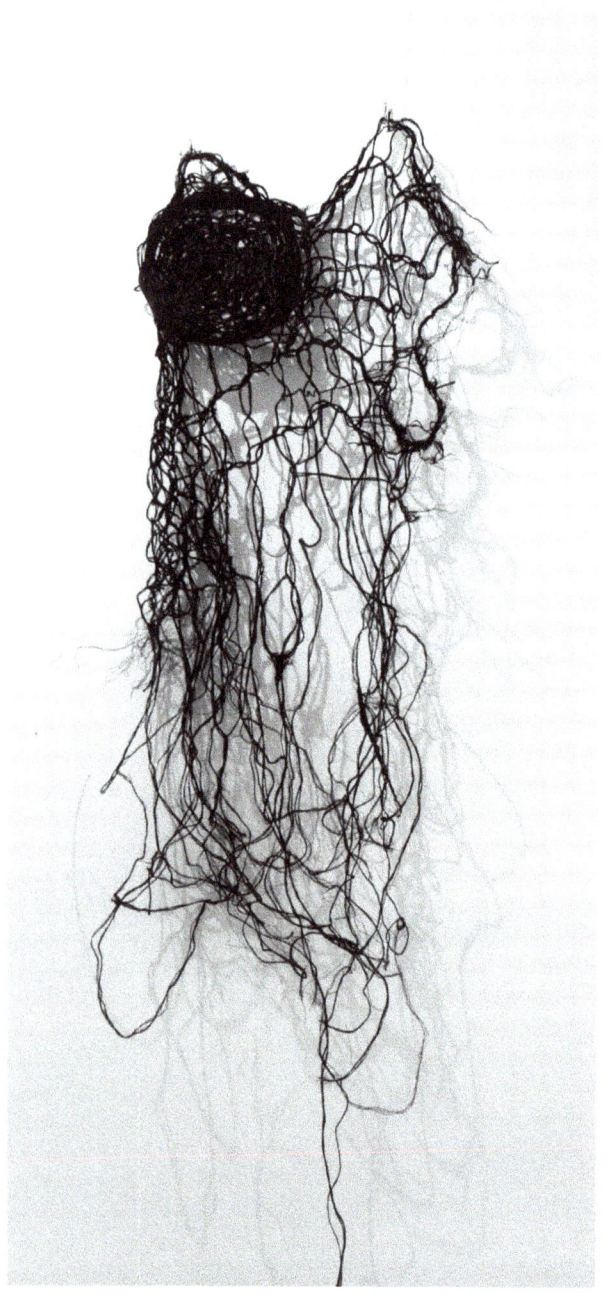

Brooke Munro loves the simple life. Her family has a working farm situated next to Morton National Park in the Southern Highlands region of NSW – with plenty of fresh air and lots of places to fossick about. Having nature at her doorstep means materials are always plentiful. There's no shortage of foliage strewn about on the bush floor around her property. For Brooke, these materials are the lifeblood of her work: found objects that when woven together make breathtaking sculptural form.

Brooke and her husband Colin work in a creative partnership named, Mr & Mrs Munro. The venture incorporates Brooke's basketry with Colin's building and fabrication skills, to produce everything from bespoke timber furniture, woven art pieces, light shades and other creative pieces. At the core their focus is sustainability as well as the creation of stunning living spaces.

Through her body of work, Brooke pays homage to what nature has tossed aside: reeds, vines, twigs, sometimes animal bone. Sculpting these materials, she feels, is a way to acknowledge their beauty and their very existence. "Whether they've fallen from trees or found on a fence, they've had their own life." It is through their use as a medium, that Brooke feels she can give them a second life, a renaissance through sculptural form.

Choosing materials for each work is a process that changes from piece to piece. "Each material

Opposite page:
Depart
Photo by Ashley Mackevicius
Fibres: Wire

This page from top right:
Omental
Photo by Ashley Mackevicius
Fibres: Paper yarn and Wire

Joanie
Photo by Ashley Mackevicius
Fibres: Wire, Horse hair

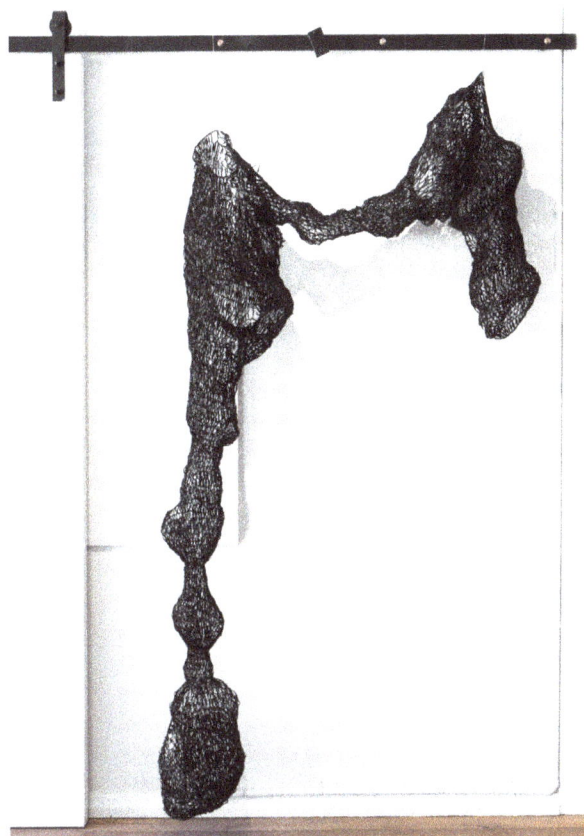

is picked for engineering or aesthetic purpose. It all has its place. Sometimes it is as simple as whatever is available." Often, Brooke will add rusted wire -she'll find pieces of it scattered about her family's property, perhaps once part of a fence or coop, now encased in a burnt orange shell.

Brooke first discovered sculptural textiles while studying a Bachelor of Creative Arts at the University of Wollongong. She learned under the artist and basketry pioneer, Virginia Kaiser. Virginia was a trailblazer of contemporary basketry in Australia, instrumental in putting the craft on the map through exhibitions and her own pre-eminent style. Sadly, Virginia passed away after a long illness in 2012. Under Virginia's direction, Brooke embraced basketry, "I found that weaving and basketry just spoke to me." These days Brooke considers herself incredibly fortunate to teach and practise basketry as a profession.

As a child Brooke would knit and crochet with her grandmother. She watched in awe at the ease with which her grandmother would work at a pattern, her hands working so fast they looked to be flowing of their own volition. "The simple pleasure of creative play was a big part of my childhood - I now find my own hands working as quickly, the same way I used to see my grandmother's." It is craft's ability to link generations through the sharing of knowledge, that Brooke sees as its most profound trait, "To see my own daughters discovering skills the way I had, it brings me the greatest joy. It's that cycle of knowledge being passed on. Basketry, links the past with the present in the same way."

For Brooke, the creative process isn't clear-cut and varies greatly with each piece, "If it's a commissioned work it has to be well planned, but often I'll begin with a material and have no clear direction in mind." Although she's never completely without resolve, 'tackling obstacles along the way can often provide new direction and a more exciting final piece'. She will sometimes use a range of techniques, some which she is new to. It's her belief that an artist's skills should always evolve, 'you never want to stagnate'. Techniques that have featured predominantly in Brooke's work are coiling, random weaving and looping.

"For me, basketry is a wonderful escape. It's about slowing down and appreciating the now. You're not thinking about tomorrow." Escapism aside, Brooke sees real magic in the way the craft allows the mind to wander. "There's always the possibility that my hands are recalling genetic memory as they work - skills held in the generations before me. Now that's magic in its truest sense," she says.

This page:
Passing
Photo by the artist
Fibres: Wire and Waratah sticks

Tripods
Photo by the artist
Fibres: Wire and Coachwood

Passage
Photo by the artist
Fibres: Wire and bone

Untitled
Photo by the artist
Fibres: Wire and found objects

Opposite page:
O
Photo by the artist
Fibres: Aluminium and steel

DELISSA WALKER

This page:
Guppy Catcher
Photo by Marc Pricop, Installation view: long water: fibre stories, 2020, Institute of Modern Art, Brisbane. Image courtesy of the artist and the Institute of Modern Art. Fibres: Guava tree, Black Palm fibre and native beeswax

Delissa Walker grew up in Mossman close to the Daintree Rainforest of north Queensland, surrounded by a diverse ecosystem dating back over 180 million years – older even than the Amazon. Like so many of her fellow artists – she was taught to weave by a doting matriarch, her grandmother, Wilma Walker. Wilma was an elder of the Kuku Yalanji people of Mossman Gorge far north east Queensland and herself an acclaimed weaving artist.

A mother of 13, her grandmother Wilma hadn't the time, unsurprisingly, to teach her own children the craft. But with Delissa it was different. The passing down of familial craft knowledge had merely skipped a generation, and in Delissa she found a pragmatic student she dubbed 'my little apprentice' to those who would see them working together.

Delissa credits her 'Nana' with teaching her and some of her cousins to weave at eight years old. Before that, at age six, she had been taught how to strip and prepare the fibres of the Black Palm for use in dilly bags and kakan baskets. The kakan baskets of northern Queensland are made with an open weave style unlike the tightly woven Dilly bag. While beautiful, the kakan style also holds historical significance for the Walker family. When Wilma was three, white authorities came to her hometown to remove indigenous children from their families. Wilma's mother hid her in a

This page:
Guppy catcher
Photo by Marc Pricop, Installation view: long water: fibre stories, 2020, Institute of Modern Art, Brisbane. Image courtesy of the artist and the Institute of Modern Art.
Fibres: Guava tree, Black Palm fibre and native beeswax

kakan basket with a seed pod to occupy her and keep her quiet – this act saved her from being forcefully separated from her family.

These days, Delissa, like her grandmother, is a much-celebrated artist and weaver. Her baskets and sculptural pieces find themselves in collections across the country: The National Gallery of Australia, The Cairns Art Gallery, and the Gallery of South Australia to name only a few. Her material of choice is the Black Palm (*Normanbya normanbyi*) – a native hardy palm that only grows in the wet tropics of far north Queensland – the tree's leaves will darken from green to black as it matures, a unique characteristic for a palm of its genus.

It was a piece of Black Palm that her mother gifted her when she was 21 – that pushed Delissa to pick up weaving again. The gift triggered a flood of memories: of Wilma showing her the way to prepare fibres, of learning to weave the palm into form. "It all came back to me," she says, "It felt right." And so, the path from apprentice to protégé was set.

For Delissa, learning about 'country' in the Aboriginal sense has been a driving force for her work, and her life. She has travelled from the monsoonal edges of Arnhem Land, to the dusty plains of the Red Centre, and back to the crystal waters and granite boulders of Mossman Gorge, learning from elders about the land, the sea, and of the seasons. It is this connection to country that Delissa weaves into each piece, creating contemporary art infused with an ancestral past.

To weave her magic, Delissa will use the end of the Black Palm leaf, the bit just before the trunk. She will use a mussel shell to strip it back, removing gunk and dirt. The process requires the whole tree to be felled, but none of it is wasted. Its wood, she dubs 'aboriginal steel' is given to her cousins for use in building and artefacts such as clapsticks, an Indigenous percussion instrument.

When the Black Palm is unavailable, she will use Lomandra, a native grass, although she 'finds it slippy' and harder to control than her staple.

Black Palm, once a flourishing species of the far north, is now threatened by habitat destruction caused by development and logging. Delissa's goal is to plant one hundred - she and a friend have already planted ten.

Delissa has a professional aim to sell a piece of artwork in every state, and she is almost there. Most recently she sold five pieces to the National Gallery of Victoria. She also teaches her craft at workshops. "It's in my blood," she explains. "I also like the stable income."

These days when she's not teaching, she will focus on other forms outside of baskets, choosing non-traditional styles such as contemporary sculptures, wall hangings and mats. She's begun using non-traditional raffia, also made from palm, but different in texture to the Black Palm she has grown up with.

Like the teachings of her elders, weaving provides Delissa, a grounding to place and past. Each of her pieces, traditional or not, is shrouded in historical context as well as her own story. And in every artwork, a piece of Wilma lives on.

Opposite page:
Kakan (Basket)
Photo by Shannon Brett
Fibres: Black Palm, Lawyer cane and native beeswax

This page:
Kakan (Basket)
Photo by Shannon Brett
Fibres: Black Palm, Lawyer cane and native beeswax

FLEUR BRETT

Fleur's practice is very diverse as she experiments with a wide variety of materials and mediums and works across two and three dimensions from printmaking and collage through to large scale woven installations. Having started work as a graphic designer for television, she then studied printmaking and finally discovered and fell in love with sculpture.

It was during her Honours year, while studying Sculpture at Melbourne's RMIT University that she began her foray into the world of textiles. While experimenting with traditional French knitting techniques, she first used recycled industrial data cable to create forms that held shape. She used the same technique for the basis of one of her seminal works **The Gathering**; a large-scale installation of abstract forms made of coloured cable, set starkly, though wonderfully against the backdrop of nature. The cable is said to represent communication in the modern age.

After graduating, Fleur picked up random weave, coiling and twining techniques from basketry workshops with Basketmakers of Victoria (BOV). She was celebrated as an artist in residence at the Australian Tapestry Workshop and added to her growing repertoire with skills picked up from indigenous artists through the Koori Heritage Trust and Close the Gap indigenous programs. What has attracted her to these environments and to the textile field is the generosity of the (mostly female) practitioners with their incredible

skills and humility. The opportunity to work alongside other creative people in these community settings and share ideas and knowledge continues to sustain Fleur's practice.

Her work **Blackbird Girl, Kooky Tree & Bug Bush** was inspired both by the idea of a memory basket and a flip flap book she had as a child where the bodies of animals became interchangeable. The work itself, made using buttonhole stitch and pieces of fabric and recycled cardboard can be taken apart and reassembled in a combination of ways, like a 3D woven puzzle.

Opposite page:
Tribal #1 (The Fan Club)
Photo by Theresa Harrison
Fibres: Woven crepe paper streamers with Palembang cane

This page:
Shelter
Photo by Fleur Brett
Fibres: Woven reclaimed data cable

Her piece **Shelter** explores poverty and homelessness in her hometown. It began as a drawing of a homeless man sleeping in a Melbourne Park, that soon developed into a tapestry. The final sculpture, made of data cable and Dymo tape woven around steel, presents a resting figure enshrined in a tent.

Fascinated with the tribal nature of sports clubs and their followers, Fleur used football fans as a basis for her series **The Fan Club**. For the final piece, using the twining technique, she used crepe paper streamers woven around cane as a visual celebration of the pre-game football banner. For research she bunkered down with Western Bulldogs Official Fan Club as they made a banner for the weekly game.

In her work **The Spinster and Wonder(full) Woman** Fleur explores female identity through a reimagining of the term spinster. The pieces, made from crepe paper and carved apple wood, splay out like a colourful butterfly. In keeping with this theme, Fleur chose apple wood as a material to symbolize Eve's original sin. She enrolled in a woodworking course to learn how to carve it.

Fleur's process is methodical, and always evolving. She dives deeply into each project like a method actor on assignment. Her large-scale installation and sculptural work is said to leave viewers transfixed – a true testament to her skill as an artist and storyteller.

Opposite page:
The Spinster & Wonder(full) Woman
Photo by Theresa Harrison
Fibres: Woven crepe paper streamers & cane

This page:
Fleur at work
Photo by Page McLean
Working on woven figure

Blackbird Girl, Kooky Tree & Bug Bush
Photo by Theresa Harrison
Fibres: Recycled clothing, cardboard and raffia

HELLE JORGENSEN

Helle describes herself as an 'investigator of materials and form'. At the core, she is an explorer, driven by a palpable curiosity for the natural world. Her authentic essence permeates from every one of her creations in which you can capture her sense of humour.

Helle's studio is an inviting space, in parts a wonderful ramshackle of books, artworks and creative projects. On closer inspection, you see there's a clinical order amidst the pandemonium of colour and shape. Ceramics and hand-woven small objects adorn a small table, placed in a perfect assemblage. There are bright crochet pieces in every hue of the colour wheel. Nearby there's string she's effortlessly made from natural fibres. Everything has its rightful place.

Born in Denmark, Helle arrived in Australia as a teenager. She lived in Sydney before relocating to Northern NSW in 2009. These days, home is a small acreage in the Tweed Valley where she lives with her partner and until recently their pet Hereford cow, Harriet. The area is a subtropical oasis, wedged between a postcard coastline to the east and lush rainforest country to the west. It's laden with natural materials she can use in her work.

Helle studied Biology at university. As a graduate, she worked in marine biology, observing populations of blue-green algae. She later spent time working in the field of cancer research before redirecting her curiosity toward arts and horticulture. As an artist, her work spans a variety of styles and media, from organic 3D forms to the bold freshness of mid-century modern.

Helle also believes that basketry provides an important bond and connection to previous generations and other cultures. "Basketry techniques are ancient; they're part of the traditional material cultures of people worldwide. To simply sit and create using one's hands gives one space to think deeply and with clarity."

In her works, Helle predominantly uses local plant species, indigenous and exotic, such as Bangalow Palm (*Archontophoenix cunninghamiana*), Soft Twig Rush (*Baumea rubiginosa*), Mat-Rush (*Lomandra hystrix*), Common Rush (*Juncus usitatus*) and Cumbungi (*Typha orientalis*). She also finds a use for Cat's Claw Creeper (*Dolichandra unguis-cati*), a weed of national significance. She'll often incorporate found objects, ceramics and animal

Opposite page:
Wearable Life Insurance (a diverse policy)
Photo by Michelle Eabry
Fibres: plant material, clay, wood, found objects and wooden hooks

This page, left to right:
L-Circumspection
Photo by Michelle Eabry
Fibres: Bangalow Palm inflorescence & Lomandra
R-Circumspection
Photo by Michelle Eabry
Fibres: Hemp bark & found bones

Lofty Thoughts Processor
Photo by Michelle Eabry
Fibres: Bangalow Palm inflorescence & waxed cotton thread, hemp & wooden hook

hair (horse, cow, pig and human) into her works. Looping, twining, coiling and random weaving are the basketry techniques she commonly uses.

In recent years, Helle has discovered a love for Banana fibre. Near her home, the Banana is grown as an agricultural crop and is celebrated with an annual Banana Festival. Each year at the festival, someone is crowned the Banana Queen (an esteemed title Helle has yet to receive). With raw materials locally plentiful, Helle set out to weave the fibre itself.

With her first introduction to the Banana fibre, she says, "I knew it was used as a weaving material in other subtropical places but had no idea of how to process it." True to form, she spent a lot of time researching, developing and refining her technique. From her research, Helle discovered Basho-Fu, an acclaimed woven cloth made from Basho (the indigenous Banana plant of Okinawa, Japan). This stunning material was

Clockwise from top left:
Tableau 1
Photo by Michelle Eabry
Fibres: Clay, driftwood, hemp bark, plant material & hog hair

Tableau 2
Photo by Michelle Eabry
Fibres: Clay, hemp bark, plant material, horse hair & waxed cotton thread

Tableau 5
Photo by Michelle Eabry
Fibres: Clay, hemp bark, plant material, horse hair & waxed cotton thread

Tableau 4
Photo by Michelle Eabry
Fibres: Clay, driftwood, hemp bark, plant material & waxed cotton thread

predominantly made for use in traditional kimonos during the seventeenth century, and Okinawa is known as one of the few places in the world that produces it. The material is time-consuming to make (up to 3 months), but once mastered creates a supple, breathable fabric perfect for warmer climates. It is often dyed in bright, natural hues and delicately patterned. Enthralled by the fabric and the process behind it, Helle travelled to Okinawa to learn firsthand how to process the fibre.

In Okinawa, Helle obtained an artist residency where

she learned to harvest, dye and weave Basho-Fu using traditional techniques. It was on a visit to a local workshop that she met the cultural icon, Toshiko Taira, a woman credited with single-handedly keeping the craft alive after it all but disappeared following the Battle of Okinawa during the Second World War. Toshiko, now in her 90s, was one of only a few who knew the technique and ensured it was revived. Through her, the traditional techniques of the women who began the process hundreds of years ago were passed down to others - and live on to this day.

Helle continues to investigate her creative endeavours and is constantly producing new interesting work.

JESS LEITMANIS

For many years Jess Leitmanis would pick microplastics and polystyrene from the sands of her local shoreline. Inspired by the photographic works of Chris Jordan (USA), she would use these bits of plastic debris as focal points for ink drawings. From growing up on Victoria's surf coast to now living in the beach mecca, that is New South Wales's Byron Bay, there has never been a shortage of shorelines to amble along, or artificial rubble to stumble across.

It was from discovering pieces of strewn rope on these beach walks that Jess first felt compelled to create three-dimensional form. Lured by the tactility and texture of each piece, she began to conjure sculptural ideas. It was at this juncture that her passion for woven objects was first realised. Throughout her career, Jess has not only sourced material close to home, she's travelled to beach clean-ups with various environmental organisations, retrieving rope from some of the remotest coastlines of Australia.

For Jess, rope's allure lies in its journey; and the story it tells of our modern world, its systems and repercussions and of our human footprint through the ages. Rope, even at its simplest, she sees as reflexive, 'a vehicle for self-reflection for society'. Of weaving as a medium, she says, "I love that there is an element of surrender with it, because the hidden quirks and kinks of the old rope will influence the finished form."

Opposite page, clockwise from top right:
Photo by the artist unless otherwise stated
Tasmanian Wilderness World Heritage Area - Southwest National Park, (Severely) photodegraded marine debris rope, Process *(Photo by the Ben Leitmanis)*, **Rope Preparation, Busy Hands**

This page:
Spouts from Which to Drink, Circa 200 C.E.
Photo by the artist
Fibres: Salvaged marine debris rope and fishing line

Born into a creative family where artistic nuance was understood and nurtured, Jess seemed destined to work in the creative space. She studied design and worked in graphics for many years, honing her creative sensibilities through a commercial framework - something she doesn't reflect on adversely, and continues today. Describing her focus shift from designer to artist, Jess says she was prepared to throw down the gauntlet to follow her creative vision, "When I committed to exploring my own creative whims, I was prepared to dive deep, and quickly."

She discovered established artists such as Fiona Hall, Magdalena Abakanowicz, and was itching to develop a substantial body of work of her own. First and foremost, she felt an immense gratitude to the First Nations People – and indigenous cultures world over – for originating and refining basketry and weaving techniques that are still used today.

For Jess, the weaving process provides catharsis. Like other basketry and weaving artists, she describes the repetition of movement, of hand and fibre, as meditative. When working on a project for long periods - often for hours on end - she says, simply, "time ceases to exist." Inspiration for each project, she tells, comes from observing

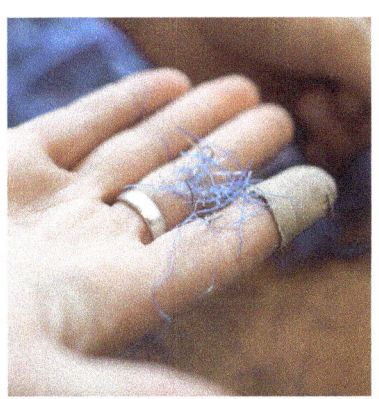

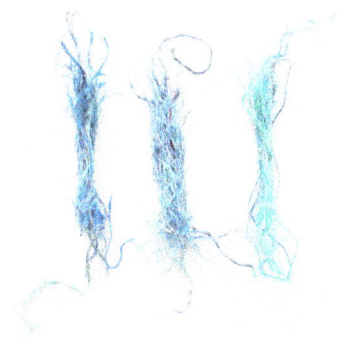

people and their interactions with the living world – how they use it, discard it, replace it, and so on. It's within this symbiotic relationship that she sees the finer details: the social structures, the physical formations, the movements, lights and textures.

Jess will begin the making process by arranging rope by colour. Most of it, she says, is severely faded and in advanced stages of degradation. She painstakingly unravels the fibres of woven plastic to expose a variation of hue and texture. It is at this stage that she says the rope becomes, 'a visual reflection of a passage of time'. Due to the photodegradation of the material and the airborne fibres it releases through processing, Jess must wear a face mask to protect her lungs from microplastics. If working in an enclosed space, she will use an industrial air filter, ensuring that dusts is disposed of in a way that is safest for the environment.

Once the rope is processed, Jess will use basic weaving techniques to ensure the material remains a focal point. "I want the rope's character to stand out. When I make solid coil vessels, the looping stitch is fishing line. This means the stitch work is secondary to the coiled material itself." She explains further. Her works are almost always made using a coil technique and a double twist technique, of which she adds, "I taught myself techniques through observing woven objects, so I don't know the exact technical terms." Not being a stickler for the rules is undoubtedly what makes each of her pieces such a spectacle - she will welcome imperfections as she works, believing they add character. "If I'm too controlling," she says, "my work loses life."

Jess often thinks about the dynamic between artist and viewer. As an artist, she says she's always wanting to start a dialogue through her work. "Ultimately, I want people to have their own relationship with each piece, and maybe be inspired to view the world a little differently

afterwards," she reflects. An abstract thinker herself, she doesn't mind if the dialogue is subjective. If it's there, she says, her job is done.

Opposite page:
Detail of Cocoon of Convenience 1200 B.C.E.
Photo by the artist
Fibres: Salvaged marine debris rope and fishing line

Cocoon of Convenience 1200 B.C.E.
Photo by the artist
Fibres: Salvaged marine debris rope and fishing line

This page:
Cloak of Invisibility: Bleaching Part 1 Circa 5th Century
Photo by the artist
Fibres: Salvaged marine debris rope and fishing line

JUSTINE WELLMAN

Long before basketry, it was ceramics that stoked Justine's creative juices, "I would dig clay as a kid, roll it into beads and fire it in our potbelly stove." After high school, Justine studied Visual Arts at the University of Newcastle, NSW. Then after taking a break to have her first child, she returned to study Ceramics at Bomaderry TAFE, "I immediately fell in love with it." But soon it was another passion that stirred her to return to study, and this was horticulture. For 15 years she worked with plants, running a nursery and cultivating her own rural block. She'd had five children and was resigned to the fact that her identity as Justine the artist would be confined to a distant memory.

On her 40th birthday, Justine gifted herself a 2-day weaving workshop held by Lissa de Sailles; a small act that had a profound impact on the course of her life. "I was immediately woven into the basketry spell." From this, the dormant flame of artistic creativity was ignited.

"I'm captivated by the ancient art of basketry, it seems something quite magical and primal about it. It takes my passion and understanding of plants to another level."

Her basketry formations are sometimes functional, sometimes sculptural - mostly made from plant material she gathers from nearby, "I search out plants with contrasting colours, plants like Red Cordyline and Ponytail Palm are a great combination." She likes to experiment

with different grasses, collecting throughout the seasons to show difference of colour. "I collect Watsonia in winter, when the leaves turn to a gorgeous rust. It's a matter of waiting and watching over time to see how the plants fade."

Her list of preferred plant material includes: Gymea Lily (*Doryanthes excelsa*), Variegated Carex (*Carex morrowii*), Variegated Arundo (*Arundo donax*) and Tall Spike-Rush (*Eleocharis sphacelata*), to name a few. All are hardy plants that take a toll on her hands through the weaving process so when she makes her own cordage, she'll often make 50-metres worth in one sitting. She will experiment with her rope's thickness, oscillating from thin to thick and chunky. "The difference in thickness gives more variation visually, as the way I construct is very simple. It can make a piece uneven and go off-centre if I'm not careful to adjust the balance."

Opposite page:
Ancient Urn
Photo by the artist
Fibres: Philodendron sheath, Ponytail Palm & waxed linen thread

This page:
Gumnut Pods
Photo by the artist
Fibres: Red Cordyline, Ponytail Palm & waxed linen thread

Justine will weave other materials into her work. She likes to use denim sourced from charity shops and looks for interesting patterned materials. She's also known to use bits of washed up rope and seaweed which she says can be tricky to work with. "It can be slimy and likes to break easily, but it dries hard and with a nice salty patina."

As a ceramicist and weaving artist, Justine sees a wonderful synergy between both her crafts. "I just love the natural poetry between grass and clay," she says, and she'll often fuse both in her work. If using clay in a woven sculpture, she will start with a ceramic vessel that she has made small holes around the rim. She will use waxed linen thread to begin coiling, using a blanket stitch. With each piece she says, "It's not purely ceramics or purely basketry, but they both belong together, separate pieces would not make sense by themselves."

Justine lives with her husband and her children in a coastal town three hours south of Sydney. She manages to create her art somewhere amidst the busyness of life as artist, partner and mother. She has plans on taking her work to a professional level, by spending more time in her recently built studio and researching for grants and art prizes so she can immerse herself and continually develop more art.

Opposite page:
Shh She-oaks
Photo by the artist
Fibres: Red cordyline leaves, Lomandra longifolia, casuarina needles and waxed linen thread

This page:
She Sells She-oaks
Photo by the artist
Fibres: Casuarina needles (She-oak) and waxed linen thread

KYLIE CALDWELL

Kylie is a Bundjalung woman and first learnt how to weave when she organised workshops for a group of girls through the Casino 'Wake Up Time Group' with teachers Margaret Torrens, Janelle Duncan and Theresa Bolt. She understood that the weaving was engaging for the girls - they would sit together and learn the craft while chatting and feeling connected.

This was the start of her journey into weaving and with her enthusiasm and eagerness she then progressed from making her baskets as homeware pieces to basketry from an arts perspective. This work was valued very differently and as basketmaking really drew her in, she kept playing and exploring with shapes and fibres. She incorporates local indigenous plants such as Buchie Rush, Lomandra, long leafed Pandanas and also includes raffia.

Making baskets was also a way she could explore culture. In 2016 she participated in the Encounters Scholarship Program with the Australia National Museum which allowed her access to archival and ancestral bags.

Kylie said this gave her a 'tangible aspect of her culture'.

"The experience had a profound effect on me. The artefacts are a connection to my culture, a record of my people and place, a source of culture, a way to heal, a way to learn; they are more than keepsakes.

Opposite page:
Tidda's
Photo by Kate Holmes
Fibres: Bangalow Palm spathe

This page:
I'm Still Standing
Photo by Kate Holmes
Fibres: Buchie Rush, inflorescence, Japanese string & metal frame

Opposite page:
Our Mountains Have Stories
Photo by Kate Holmes
Fibres: Buchie Rush, Pandanus, Lomandra dyed with native plants

This page:
Jullum Nyabay Gilamahla
Photo by Kate Holmes
Fibres: Inflorescence, ribbon, nylon twine, metal frame

They evoke memory, feeling and stories; their energy grows within you when you see them."

In 2017 Kylie won the Clarence Valley Indigenous Art Award at Grafton Regional Gallery. Through this she produced an eclectic collection of work for her solo **Woven Dreams** exhibition in 2020 of fibre work using the coiling technique. The exhibition represents the connections with family … sisters and aunties, culture, exploring connections of basketry and the environment …. drought, flood and bushfires.

She talks about the need for sisters whether they be blood sisters or an emotional connection - chats, cuppas and supporting each other throughout our lives.

Kylie shares that "Over the years of facilitating and participating in weaving workshops with various women and young girls, we have rediscovered the value in matriarchal bonding while sharing and supporting each other. Weaving has been the catalyst to enable these collective gatherings and opportunities to share stories."

MARION GAEMERS

Opposite page:
White Coral
Photo by the artist
Fibres: Beach rope and net

This page:
Lost Antiquities
Photo by the artist
Fibres: Beach rope and net

Marion Gaemers has always been a creative thinker, an existence most makers can relate to. "I don't really have a life other than being creative," she says – as is evident in her sizeable body of work spanning three decades. It's been a long time since her first group exhibition somewhere in the late 1980's - and she hasn't stopped since, carving an impressive creative path with her distinct version of contemporary expressionist sculpture.

Marion considers herself a traditionalist when it comes to the craft of basketry. She uses the ancient technique of weaving natural fibres into form – although that's where the convention ends. Her sculptural pieces, some large-scale installations - each take on a contemporary life of their own. It is this dichotomy of old and new that Marion believes is relevant to all basketmakers of today. "Working with found materials and using traditional techniques ties us to the people of the past," she says. And it is this connection of past and present that has been a driving force behind her assigning basketry as her craft of choice.

Having a partiality for the ephemeral, Marion has often made installations that are disbanded once an exhibition is over. It is this impermanence that connects her art to the natural subjects it so often represents. One such work, **Journeys**, won the main artistic award in 2009 at Townsville's biennial sculpture festival, Strand Ephemera –

Opposite page:
Pods - detail
Photo by the artist
Fibres: Mat-Rush (Lomandra)

This page:
Pods
Photo by the artist
Fibres: Mat-Rush (Lomandra)

one of Australia's biggest sculpture events. Marion has been featured in the event for over twenty years, bar one.

Like many makers, artistic collaboration has always been a motivator for making and exhibiting. Throughout her career, Marion has shared her skills with others whenever she could and enjoys travelling to other communities for this reason – often soaking up local knowledge herself, learning how to use different localised materials and skills.

Marion is a member of Fibres and Fabrics, Townsville's textile group which has also been a source of collaboration and her own artistic nurturement.

Back when she began exhibiting, the materials she used would change with the seasons. "If plant materials were in abundance, I'd see what I could find and start from there." If it could be used straight from the plant with little processing, she explains, "Well, that was a win." Marion's most used medium back then was mostly raw plant material she collected around the place. Nature, she says, would act as artistic director: dictating the technique and the style of her finished work.

These days Marion is more likely to incorporate rubbish she finds strewn along a beach into her work, a medium she uses as a creative representation of our problematic relationship with the natural environment. This change she puts down to becoming a part of the Ghost Net Movement, an organisation that works with indigenous rangers to find discarded fishing nets, repurposing them for artwork and basketry projects. To date, since its inception in 2004, Ghost Net has found and repurposed 14,000 abandoned, discarded or lost fishing nets that would otherwise cause harm to oceanic ecosystems and wildlife. Marion often works collaboratively with Lynnette Griffiths creating large installations of work in net and rope. Together they also collaborate with Erub Arts, an arts centre on Darnley Island in the Torres Straits.

Marion attributes many for influencing her over the years. Landscape artists, Andy Goldsworthy and Chris Drury are some, metal sculpture artist, Bronwyn Oliver is another. There are many more people who have kept her motivated throughout her artistic career; she credits people she's taught back in the early days, also others who encouraged her to exhibit, and people she has met at gatherings and workshops along the way.

Marion's passion for her craft that has seen her exhibit locally and nationally almost continuously since her first exhibition shows no sign of waiving, "I always make work for an exhibition if I am asked," she says. Her enchanting sculptural works live on, so it seems.

MAVIS WARRNGILNA GANAMBARR

This page:
Mavis working on a basket in progress
Photo by Alex Warland
Fibres: Pandanas

Mavis Warrngilna Ganambarr sees weaving as a story, a very important story that once heard, must be told and passed on so that it is never forgotten. Mavis first heard this story from her grandmother, Djuluka, many years ago starting with a lesson on how to make bush string from the stringy bark tree. She learnt which plants to use for dying fibres, and how to coil her own baskets using local plants.

It took a long time for Mavis to learn the art of weaving, "It was so hard," she says of learning the craft from her beloved grandmother. However long it took, she is now celebrated as one of the most renowned weavers in Australia. Acknowledged as a senior fibre artist in Arnhem Land, she has exhibited nationwide, notably in the National Gallery of Australia, the National Gallery of Victoria which has acquired her works, and the Art Gallery of South Australia to name a few. Most recently she has been awarded the Australian Design Centre's Living Treasures, Master of Australian Craft exhibition.

Mavis was born in 1966 by the banks of a creek in Matamata, North East Arnhem Land. It's a small homeland with just a few families living there. The traditional custodians, the Yolngu thrived for thousands of years before English occupation – their culture rich with art representing their clan and country.

At nine, Mavis moved to Galiwinku Elcho Island - Galiwin'ku as it's traditionally called - where she went to a nearby bush school. The first day she cried as she knew no-one and she didn't know how to read and write. The next day a Balanda (non Yolngu) student sat next to her and said "Don't worry I'll be your friend," and they are still friends all these years later. In her adult life she started her family there and has five children and nine grandchildren. She still visits her hometown regularly although she must fly to get there. "I love it. It's my birthplace," she says of her visits back to Matamata. Sometimes she stays for a long time.

This page:
Basket 2006
Photo permission Arts NT / ReCoil

©Mavis Galikali Warrngilna Ganambarr / Copyright Agency, 2022
Fibres: Pandanas and natural earth pigment

Growing up, she lived in awe of her father, Mowarra Ganambarr, a well-known bark painter, "He was respected by the Yolngu because he had great wisdom," she says. She would watch him prepare bark ready for painting, a process that could take weeks. "It was a lot of work," she emphasises of her father's artistic process. "I miss him." Like her father, Mavis will also use ochre pigments in her pieces and is one of the few women to do this.

As far as materials go, Mavis will pick local pandanus. She splits the prickly fibre, then boils it with dye-plants such as Djundum, a small hardy tree whose roots create a vivid sun yellow. Once rendered and dried, the fibres become a soft pliable thread. With it, she will coils baskets, twines mats, creates fish sculptures, loops bags and creates very fine beautiful jewellery adding feathers, tiny shells and fine string.

Mavis incorporates traditional methods into her work passed down by her grandmother and her father and incorporates her own sense of design that makes her work distinctive and unique. She is a prolific artist constantly producing a myriad of new work.

For Mavis, teaching is a vital part of keeping weaving traditions alive. She teaches the young people in her community hoping that they too will pass it down to their children. She is proud of her daughter, Judith who makes baskets just as she does, and who she hopes will keep the story alive.

Opposite page:
Bag
©Mavis Galikali Warrngilna Ganambarr / Copyright Agency, 2022

This page:
Owls
©Mavis Galikali Warrngilna Ganambarr / Copyright Agency, 2022
Fibres: Pandanas

NICOLE ROBINS

Nicole Robins's interest in basketry began in midlife. Working as a Couple and Family therapist she felt that she had been searching for a creative outlet for some time. As a plant lover and gardener she tried a basketry workshop with Meri Peach at the Sydney Botanical Gardens in 2012. "It was a decision made on a whim," she says, "but I haven't stopped since."

On picking up the craft, Nicole soon realised that through most of her life, she has been drawn to basketry and textural art forms. She lived in Latin America for most of her 20s and has since continued to travel whenever she can with her family. "It felt like I had been looking at basketry and weaving and craft around the world for a long time. I am drawn to the artistry and colour, and how these living arts relate so closely to people's lives, especially women's."

For nearly twenty years, Nicole has lived in Sydney's inner west - once a working-class municipality but now quite gentrified and home to a vibrant café and arts scene. Nearly all her materials are gathered or grown in the local area. "The sustainable element of my work brings me great joy. I like to use whole, recognisable fibres whenever I can. Indigenous plants, exotics and even 'weeds'. I use basketry techniques that will showcase the beautiful fibres, rather than the other way around." The vast diversity of Sydney's plant life mean that she is never short of inspiration. As a green thumb, she's not afraid

Opposite page:
Leaning Tower of Plantyness
Photo by Katie Cluelow
Fibres: Dracaena draco, Agave attenuata, Cordyline, Dracaena marginata, Yucca filamentosa

This page:
Wall Urn
Photo by Katie Cluelow
Fibres: Dracaena draco, Pandanus, Iris, Bromeliad, Gymea Lily, Sanseviera, Bangalow Palm inflorescence, Yucca filamentosa, Cordyline, Agave attenuata

to get her hands dirty growing and seeking her materials – often using leaves and plant waste left discarded in the street.

While plants bring inspiration, so too do the human elements of life that surround her – ideas for her weaving forms are drawn from all domains of life – how people live and what they choose to have around them to give their environment beauty and meaning.

Her artwork style is changeable. Generally she sees a connection to the basketry 'vessel' yet most pieces are not functional baskets. Many are wall sculptures. Her main interest is in trying to create shapes and work that she hasn't seen before. Many look very organic in shape - she hopes the connection to their original fibre story and 'roots' is still a strong presence.

In recent years she has been drawn to the idea of hanging work – baskets, flat pieces, wall sculptures and pendants. "I like the idea of bringing the natural world into our interior landscapes, of beautifying and texturising our living and working spaces."

Nicole takes issue with the way that artistic value often doesn't account for the time it takes to create. "Not everyone realizes that all baskets are handmade and that the gathering, drying, soaking and weaving process takes considerable time. It's a slow craft." Nicole readily embraces the ideas espoused by the slow craft movement where the process and the artisan are equally valued.

A long-time feminist, Nicole has been passionate about women's development projects, which help women earn a liveable income through art and craftwork. In her 2019 exhibition **Totes Serious... who made your bag?** she explored the idea of the humble natural fibre tote, now seen as a fashion staple. "There's been a greenwashing aspect where handmade woven bags are being

This page and opposite page work from 'Totes Serious' exhibition 2019, photos by Katie Cluelow except Easing Restrictions photo by Nicole Robins.

This page:
Easing Restrictions - *Fibres: Dracaena marginata*

Opposite page, clockwise from top left:
Agave Attenuata - *Fibres: Agave attenuata*
Philodendron - *Fibres: Philodendron*
Spring Nest - *Fibres: Jacaranda leaf stems, Dracaena draco, Agave attenuata*
Dracaena Draco Wall Tote - *Fibres: Dracaena draco*

used in fashion shoots everywhere. They have come to signify ethical, handmade, and of course 'natural' by their very appearance. At the same time, their makers are invisible. These bags are often made in poorer countries where makers, mostly women, aren't paid a living wage." She calls for far greater transparency in the fashion supply chain. "Consumers have more power than they think when it comes to helping artisans and craftspeople to earn a reasonable living from their work. We need to feel comfortable asking lots of questions about products that we buy."

Nicole identifies as a non-Indigenous Australian weaver. "I am extremely privileged to have grown up around some of the most beautiful fibre art in the world. The learning and inspiration from being able to see, and even pick up and examine exquisite work from Australia's First Nations' makers are immeasurable." Out of respect for these cultures she aims to appreciate rather than copy. "I don't use materials or designs or even language which I think is intrinsic to the fibre art made by Indigenous artists here. Of course, this line will always be a fine and nuanced one that artists need to keep talking about here in Australia."

Nicole continues to show her work in Sydney and wider NSW, selling her pieces in galleries and through her website. If her aim is to beautify the interior space, she has certainly done just that. Her love of plant life and cultivation of local fibre shows no signs of waning. "Fibre art allows me to create an inner sanctuary that carries my love for nature inside and yet reminds us all of our fragile coexistence."

Since the pandemic and the long periods of lockdown in Sydney, being able to bushwalk and visit some of our more remote national parks in Australia has become quite a priority. The global climate crisis is a pressing concern for Nicole and like many artists she feels that she is currently grappling with how to be, and live, in this situation. Her 2021 exhibition **The Green Room** was a response to this reality.

PAULA DO PRADO

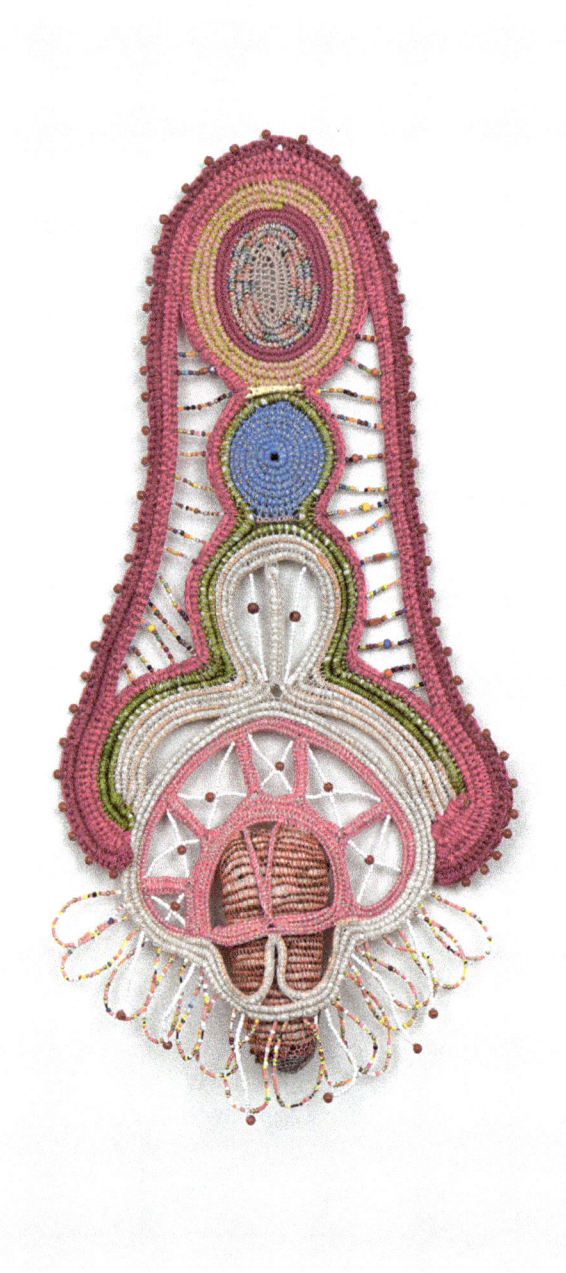

Paula do Prado's work is a deep exploration of self-identity, of cultural lineage, and of the various intersections she inhabits as a black woman. Basketry not only allows her to physically weave fibre into structure, it has also allowed her to weave the rich tapestry of her life into a vast body of work.

Born on Charrúa land (Montevideo), Uruguay, she emigrated to Australia with her parents in 1986. "As a black woman and a migrant living on stolen land, I am passionate about art and its potential as a self-liberating practice, and pathway to healing." She sees her work as a manifestation of questions and growing understanding she has, about the human condition, of existence, and of her own heritage.

Her work is layered with cultural reference – from what she describes as African diasporic traditions to South American mythology, notably ancient stories from Uruguay, Brazil and Argentina. Over time, she says her practice has evolved from research into her own genealogy. "I began to incorporate what I found out about my diverse lineages including Bantu (West African), Basque, Catalan, Portuguese and Indigenous Uruguayan heritage into my making practice."

Her love of basketry reared itself at the end of her undergraduate degree, when she won a place at a weeklong textile retreat in Orange, NSW. "I was placed in a class with Anna S. King,

Opposite page:
In Her Power 2019
Photo by Document Photography
Fibres: Crochet, coiled and beaded mixed media and fibre.

This page:
Resonance 2019
Photo by Document Photography
Fibres: Crochet, coiled and beaded mixed media and fibre.

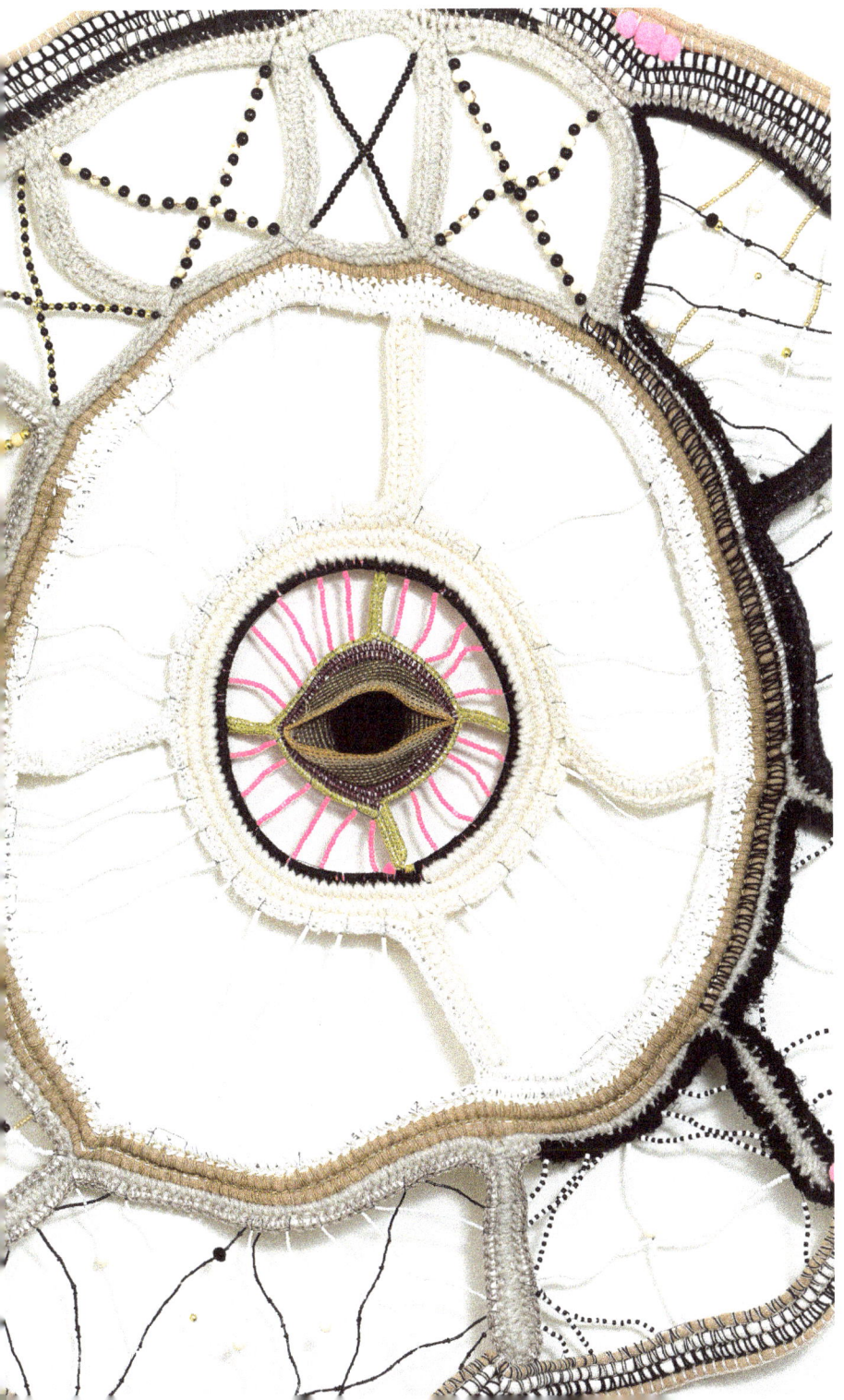

a Scottish artist who made baskets. I don't remember her teaching a particular technique, but I do remember her introducing us to her poetry and reflective writings on baskets. I remember we had discussions about the concept of the vessel and its use to hold, carry and protect - that it had an inside and an outside." Somewhere between the poetry and learnings she became hooked.

She admits that prior to this retreat, her weaving skills were basic. "Just before I had asked my mum to show me how to crochet. I only got as far as knowing how to do a long crochet chain. But Anna's class encouraged us to reflect and just do what came naturally with the materials we had, so I experimented and ended up creating three-dimensional crochet forms." From then, she continued to experiment, soon becoming one with her chosen craft.

In her work, she will use a combination of crochet and coiling together with beading, using wire to shape and give form. Outside of her own scholarly and genealogical research, inspiration for Paula comes in many forms; being in nature with her son, passing conversations, and sometimes books and film.

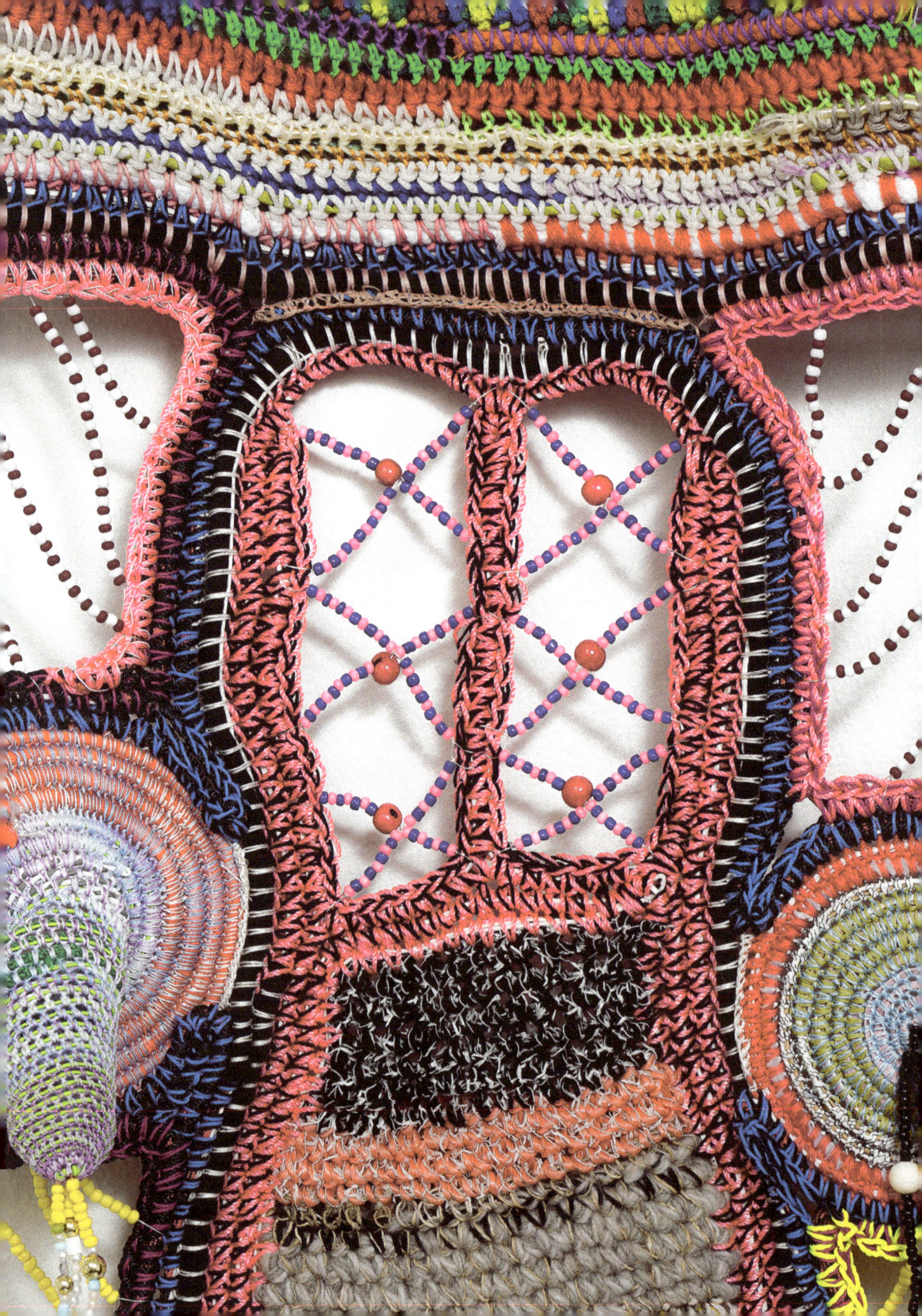

Each piece is a lengthy process, often marked by veers into other work. "I will stop working on one thing before it is finished and go off to start another or two!"

These creative pauses between works she sees as a blessing. "I love coming back to something I've put aside with a new perspective and energy. Suddenly that's when I'll figure out how to resolve it or what the next step might be." The making itself is often done in spurts over days, weeks, and months.

Paula is mostly drawn to texture and colour whether that be thread, yarn, fabric, even hair. She uses everything from cheap acrylic to fine Japanese yarn made from paper and silk. Most recently she's made a shift to using yarns made by BIWOC (Black, Indigenous and Women of Colour) and spinning her own 'art yarn' using a drop spindle. "Culturally my choice of materials comes from a making do tradition, we've always re-used and repurposed not just out of necessity, but I think just growing up with an inherent understanding of not wasting resources."

Paula comes back to the innate paradox of her craft; on one hand the practice of creating woven structure is simple, on the other it is a complex process, rich in revelation and symbolism, "It has this beautiful metaphor of pouring in all that is held within me," she explains. "The unconscious memories, the stories, the experiences, the feelings, the knowledge held in the intersection of my lineages, and transcribing these into a form that takes me back to myself."

Each basket is a journey home.

Opposite page:
Protection 2019
Photo by Document Photography
Fibres: Crochet, coiled and beaded mixed media and fibre.

This page:
Photo of the artist
Photo by Document Photography
Zita / Nudo / Knot 2019
Photo by Document Photography
Fibres: Crochet, coiled and beaded mixed media and fibre.

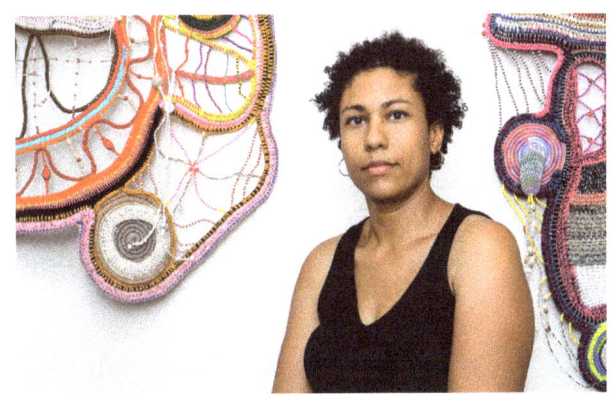

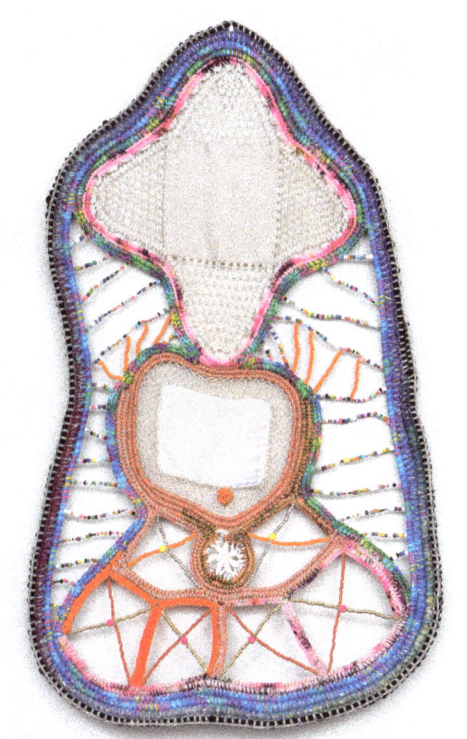

SALLY BLAKE

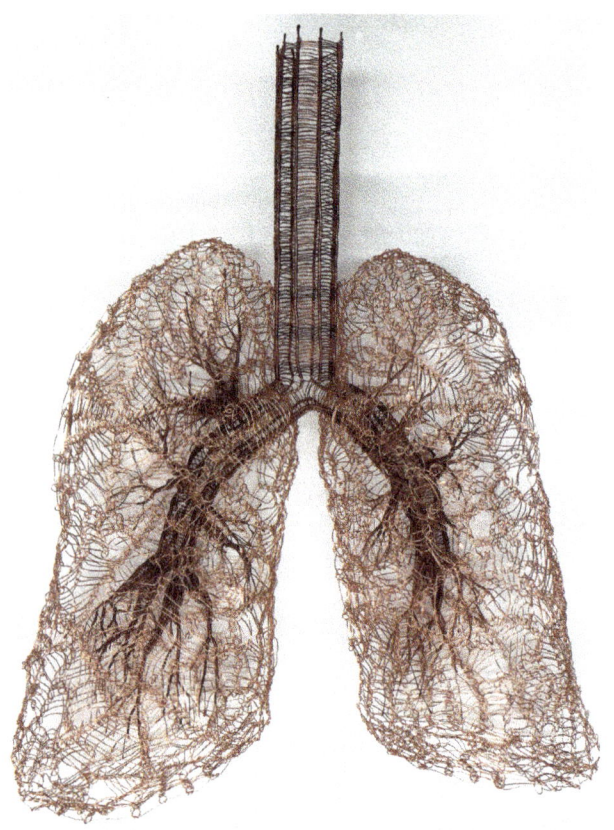

Sally Blake has always watched nature closely. As a child she would study the Prunus tree outside her window, watching as it transformed with the seasons. In nature she has always found resonances for her own experience.

Her contemporary work explores and visualises the complex interconnections between the human and natural worlds, in particular the patterning which connects humans with the natural world - cycles of death, renewal and regeneration, and patterns of an interconnected whole. In basketry, she finds ways to explore the connections between nature and self to examine this patterning.

Sally seeks inspiration from the outside world, particularly the cyclical nature of the elements, of the seasons, and of life. After her mother died someone gave her a small seedpod which became a very significant object as she mourned. She says, "This dried, skeletonised structure held a duality between life and death and a tension between vulnerability and resilience. This tiny fragile form still held its seed, and the potential for new life." She still has the seedpod 10 years later.

The seedpod inspired her to start making baskets. She started with twined copper wire as it allowed her to make forms that portrayed this tension between fragility and resilience. She liked the intricacy and strength the copper wire gave to her sculptural works. She taught herself how to patinate it, transforming it with a rich, earthy colourisation. She incorporated dyed threads - wool, silk, hemp and cotton, which she would twine around the metallic structure. With wire, she found success in the wrapping technique; and to finish her wire baskets she flattens the ends with a hammer. "It has became a unique signature in my work."

Sally explores mediums extensively; prolifically creating and experimenting until she's satisfied. Within her work, you will often see shapes within shapes. This work will often require considerable planning, as it is usually made as one continuous form.

For colour, Sally dyes her own fibres and materials with plant dye she cultivates from scratch, "I love how the colour palette always relates directly to the place in which the dye is sourced." She's undertaken two major research projects documenting natural dyes from Australian eucalyptus, "We are so lucky to have this incredible natural dye source growing in Australia." Her investigation into each species has been prolific, and generated two major research projects.

In 2016 she embarked on a study of eucalypts (*Eucalyptus*, *Angophora* and *Corymbia* species) at The Australian National Botanical Garden (ANBG), funded by The Australia Council. The project was intensive but fruitful. She collected plant materials from 230 eucalypt species, testing dyes on wool, silk and linen fabrics. She was able to create the first ever comprehensive online database of Eucalyptus dyes. The database is freely available on her website and includes recipes, fabrics and mordants.

Again, in 2018, she undertook research, supported by ArtsACT, a government arts agency, into the 27 species that grow naturally in the Australian Capital Territory (ACT). She collected

Opposite page:
Commonwealth of Breath
Photo by the artist
Fibres: Patinated Copper wire

This page:
Seep
Photo by the artist
Fibres: Aluminium wire and plant dyed wool, silk and hemp

samples from leaves and bark, as well as local anecdotes about human interactions with the eucalypts. She sees the projects as a meaningful way to link art with science. It also offered a wonderfully complex understanding of the bond between people, nature, and place.

Despite her creative passions, Sally's path to professional artist was nonlinear. After graduating high school, she chose nursing, embarking on a career in pediatrics and midwifery that spanned two decades. "I loved it," she says. But it was the insatiable pull of the creative spirit that drove her to the School of Art and Design at Australian National University (ANU) in 2004. "I realised I was always trying to make time to create," she explains. She completed her undergraduate degree with first class honours in textiles in 2007. She was awarded a doctorate in philosophy in 2015.

Sally lives in Australia's capital, Canberra, with her partner. She runs creative workshops, teaching techniques in Eucalyptus dyeing and basketry. When creating, she says she is often surprised how materials seem to take on a mind of their own, "It is one of the lovely things about it," she says. Transformations at work once again.

Opposite page:
In Memory
Photo by the artist
Fibres: Woven baskets, copper wire, plant dyed wool, silk and hemp

This page:
Multiple copper wire works
Photo by the artist
Fibres: Small baskets coiled with raffia, plant dyed wool, silk, coiled copper wire, plant dyed wool, silk and hemp.

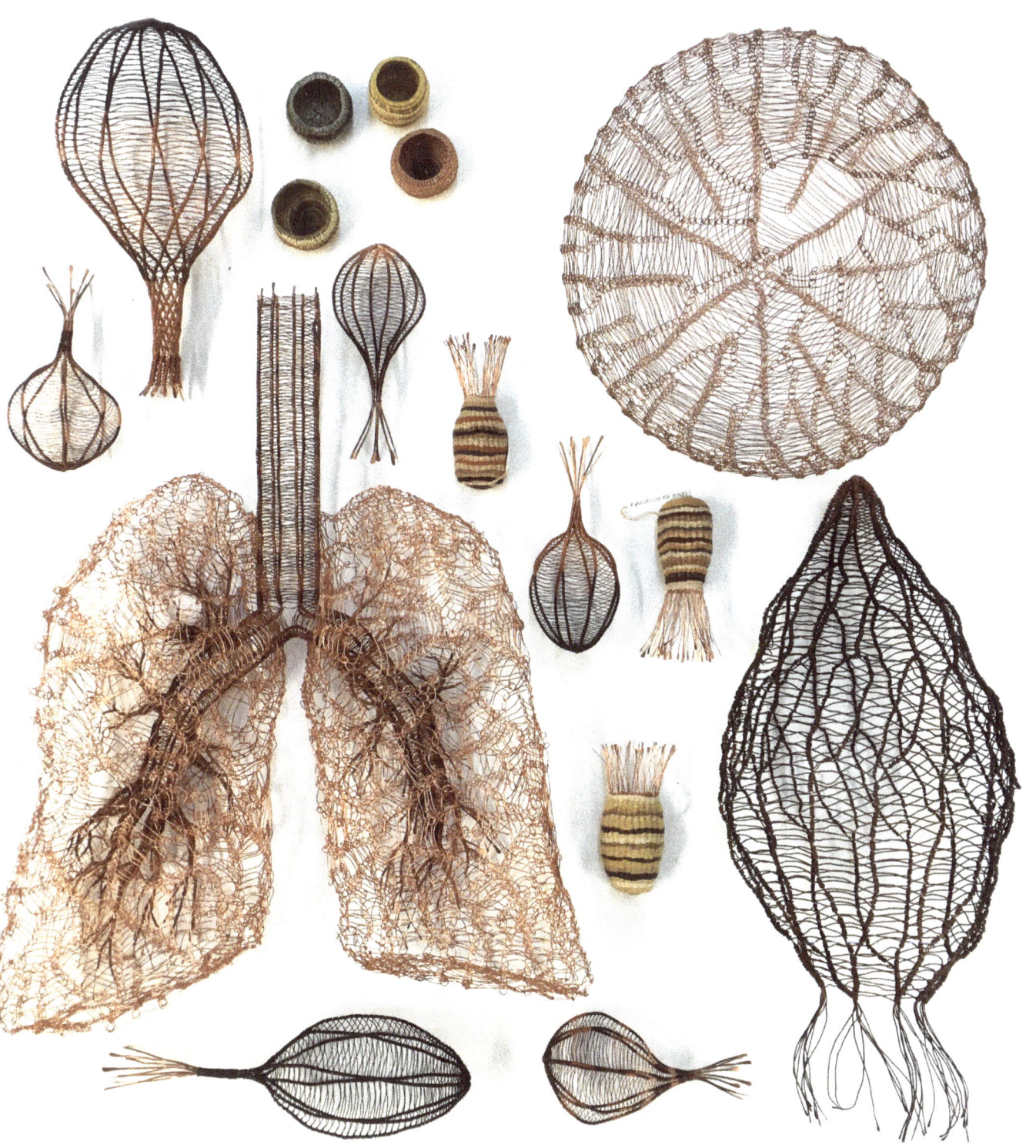

ZORA VERONA

Zora Verona proudly embraces her creative identity as an ode to her grandmothers, Zora and Verona. During the Second World War in occupied Slovenia, Zora wasn't even able to honour and christen her children with names in their own native tongue, let alone have the freedom to create works of art. The life stories of these women tell of freedoms fought for and hardships endured, so it is with reverence and gratitude that Lori Kravos chooses to create and exhibit under the name Zora Verona.

Growing up in Canada, she long held a desire to embrace a creative life and dabbled in pottery, calligraphy and crafting handmade papers from natural fibres and botanicals, yet the stigma and judgement of 'art is not a career, it is a hobby' saw her pack away her art materials and her creative dreams for decades.

Fast forward to early 2020 and with bushfires devastating and displacing billions of animals, a growing disquiet stirred by the anxiety of living through the Black Saturday fires in 2009 prompted Zora Verona to seek restoration, a sense of balance and flow that she knew could be found through creativity and art. Conflicted by the desire to create, yet not wanting to add fuel to the fire of a consumer driven society already drowning in waste, she had an epiphany as she sat at her kitchen table. She was surrounded by the answer. With Eastern Spinebills feeding from the Salvia blooms directly outside her window, a lyrebird serenade could be heard in the distance as Superb Fairy-wrens danced on the lawn and she knew then that she could not only honour her grandmothers, she could also honour the plant life and the wildlife which had been lost. So began a journey to create sustainable art made from foraged flora, fauna and found objects that honoured the art and architecture of bird nests.

Nests are layered with meaning and symbolism, from home, a sense of safety, embracing beauty in decay, to impermanence and the ephemeral. They also have the power to transport the viewer

Opposite page:
Zora in her studio
Photo by John Christie

This page:
Zora's Nest - The first nest Zora made after she had an 'epiphany' in the kitchen
Photo by John Christie
Fibres: Kunzea, lichen, moss, Eucalyptus bark, seedpods and leaves & Calamus moti 'eggs'

Opposite page, clockwise from top right:
With What is Left - the Nest of the Northern Oriole
Fibres: Plastics, net, baling twine and chaff bag threads

Master of Song - the Nest of the Song Sparrow
Fibres: Typha orientalis, Crocosmia, Acacia melanoxylon seed casings, Grevillea leaves and flowers

Small is Beautiful
Fibres: Horse hair, moss and dried herbs

Exotic fibres (weeds) from the paddocks

This page:
Testament to Resilience - the Nest of the Hoary Redpoll
Fibres: Squash vine, llama wool, feathers, dyed quails eggs

Photos by John Christie

to faraway times and lands, connecting them with the beauty of the rare and wonderful treasures of our avian world. In relation to Zora Verona's own artistic journey they are a perfect metaphor for bravery. Just like a fledgling, she has cast aside the doubts of the past that once weighed down her creative dreams to leave the nest, spread her wings, and take flight to soar with her art.

The birds themselves have also been Zora Verona's greatest teachers as she could not find anyone else creating nest sculptures in this same manner. Through the powers of observation of the birds in her own garden and researching historical nest collections in natural history museums, she felt even more inspired to tell their stories. She wanted to share the sense of wonder and awe she felt at their tenacity, determination, skill and ingenuity. How is it that birds could weave, felt, stitch and craft their myriad of creations using only beak and breast? In participating in one of the online courses offered by Craft School Oz, Baskets from the Garden, Zora Verona discovered that the nest building process and techniques of birds, from splitting, striping, and shaping, to coiling and random weave, were all echoed in human weaving traditions.

Zora Verona has also followed the birds' lead when it comes to gathering and using materials. Blessed to be nestled on the slopes of Mount Little Joe in the Yarra Valley, her wayward tangle of a garden and undulating paddocks are her 'studio storage cupboards' supplying a treasure trove of native and exotic plants as well as found objects to gather, test and trial in her sculptures. She weaves, creates and curates her nests as the birds do, using everything from plant fibres to snake skin, roots and grasses, lichen and moss, to llama wool, horse hair, bones and even plastic.

What underscores or defines Zora Verona's work is inspired by Oscar Wilde's sentiments, 'What we see and how we see it, depends on the arts that have influenced us'.

If art does affect the way we look at the world, it certainly mirrors her vision to create sustainable art that guides the viewer to recalibrate their moral compass to nature as our true north. She fears that nature is a mere afterthought, so she creates in the hope that **The Art of Nests** can change perceptions. That each nest, the bird that created it and their unique story have the power to awaken an understanding that every species is worthy of our wonder, awe and most importantly our protection.

All her materials are ethically sourced, including the eggs which hail from domestically bred birds such as quails. Carefully blown with a syringe, they can be dyed with natural plants to emulate the colours found in other bird species.

MATERIALS

You can use a myriad of materials to create sculptural basketry - only your imagination limits you.

In this section we talk about our relationship with plants and how natural it feels to create basketry forms with organic material as it has been part of innate human knowledge for millennia. Recently a basket was discovered in Israel dating back over 10,000 years. Humans have been creating these vessels since we started to collect food.

If you have already discovered the relationship with plants to vessels or sculpture, you will understand the tingle of excitement when you go on this journey of discovery. If you haven't yet embarked on this venture, you have so much to look forward to. This can become an obsession and a passion for learning about what is suitable and what you can use to create your new art piece.

With a polarising view of the plastic and textile waste that humans generate - many artists are now exploring and reusing these materials to create sculpture with innovative results. Taking ocean rope off the beach, using discarded plastics, wire from industry and textile waste gives their work a clear message about the environment and fragility of our planet.

Go and explore the materials that appeal to you, experiment and play and start your journey with enthusiasm. There are no rules just a few guidelines and tips. You will learn so much along the way.

Various plants picked for weaving
Photo by Ruth Woods

USING PLANTS

NOTE: *Common names have been used in this section - if you look for the common names in the plant list you will find the botanical names.*

If you are about to start your basketry journey using plants, you will never look at plants the same way again. If you have already started this journey, then you know how exciting that can be.

Learning about plants in relationship to basketry comes with many variables .... the climate, the environment and the seasons. Plants can look very similar but react very differently when picking, drying and preparing.

If you live in a temperate climate, you might use grasses and strappy plants such as Red Hot Poker, Daylilies, NZ Flax, various rushes and vines. If you live in the subtropics you could access Banana fibre, Palm inflorescence, Cordyline and so much more. Vines will grow in all climates and are ideal for basketry although obviously there are many different species.

There are guidelines to picking and storing plants but the best way to gain confidence is the willingness to learn through experimentation and patience. Select a few plants to dry and then create and observe.

The following section has listed some of the most common plants for basketry and of course there are countless more. Below each picture there is a guide on how to harvest, dry and moisten the plants ready for use.

Where to pick or collect

Investigate what you currently have in your garden - you may be surprised at the variety of possible fibres and stems you can use.

When walking in your neighbourhood observe what's around, make friends with your neighbours, have a chat and talk to them about plants in their garden, telling them what you do with plant fibre. People are always fascinated that you can make baskets with plants.

Talk to the gardener at the local park or botanical gardens. They often have garden waste that can be incorporated into a basket.

If you are looking for something in particular, post in a local community Facebook group and ask if anyone is pruning the plant you're looking for.

Make sure you know the local laws, check your local council about picking plants on the side of road. National Parks have strict rules about picking plants and usually it's illegal unless you have a permit.

House plants can also be a source of fibre - for example, the Yucca, Dracaena and Snake plant.

What to pick

There is a multitude of plants to pick and far too many to list in this book. You might also discover new ones that you find interesting to include in your work. Don't be afraid to try them out.

If you ever wonder whether a plant will be suitable, then look for dead leaves at the base of the plant. An ideal time is early in the morning when they're still moist from the dew or after it has rained. Scrunch the fibre in your hand and see if it stays intact - that is a good indicator.

Many people ask if they can use Agapanthus but sadly there is no fibre in the leaf and it cannot be used.

Plant fibres that are friendly and soft to your hands make working with them a pleasure. Avoid using fibres with rough edges or prickles that might give you splinters. Wear gloves if you find something rough on your hands.

Long leaf, soft fleshy plants like Daylily, Daffodil and Red Hot Poker are quite beautiful and a pleasure to work with. They rehydrate quickly with a quick soak in water.

Many grasses are ideal too. Choose the ones that are softer to touch as some can be very sharp and can cut your hands. Tussock grass is good for bulk in coiled baskets.

Numerous vines and creepers can be used for basketry. Some will give you a smooth look and others can be textural and knotty. When collecting vines, you can pull the runners out to a few metres - it's always very exciting when you find a long one.

When to pick plants

Picking plants will depend on the time of year. Plants generally die back in the winter and sprout in the spring. However, in warmer climates this is different. Observe the plants through the seasons, make notes and experiment.

In the spring you will find that various rushes pop up as well as other strappy plants. These are best picked in the summer.

Flowering plants are best picked after they have flowered and some plants are good to pick all year round.

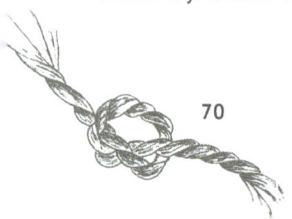

How to dry

Drying varies depending on the thickness and density of the plant and the climate where you live. A fine leaf plant like Daylily or Daffodil can take little time to dry. Plants like Arum Lilies and Irises with thicker structures will need a lot more time to dry out, sometimes months.

Depending on the shape of the leaves, make small bundles and hang for as long as they take to dry. Shorter leaves can be laid out on a table and turned regularly to allow air circulation.

Some leaves will dry on the plant or fall to the ground, these leaves can be picked and used immediately after soaking. They include Philodendron leaf sheaths, Jacaranda leaf stalks, Agave leaves, Dragon Tree leaves, Palm inflorescence and Cordyline. I'm sure you can discover more.

How to store

Storing is important and again, how you store your fibre will depend on where you live. Once they are dry store them in a laundry, utility room, garage or dry shed. You need to avoid humidity as much as possible. Some basketmakers will have fibres hanging all over the house! If you live in the tropics or a climate that has high humidity make sure you store in an airy place or the fibre will go mouldy. Use a tag and write the name of the plants as many of them look similar when dried.

How to rehydrate ready to use

Only rehydrate the materials you think you'll use. If you wet too much fibre you could waste it.

A general rule - a fine leaf fibre will not take much moisture to make it pliable to work with. Some fibres are very absorbent like Banana fibre, palm spathes, and fine leaves such as Daylilies and Daffodils which are quick to rehydrate.

Fine leaf fibres generally will need to be run under a tap or dipped in a tub of water for a couple of minutes. If the fibre is not pliable, leave for longer. If fibres are thicker, then soak up to a couple of hours and plants like Agave leaves and thick vines could take 24 hours to become pliable.

Try and use the fibre you have moistened within a day or two. If you oversoak the fibres they will absorb too much water and then shrink when they dry out.

Whatever you choose to create, don't be afraid to make mistakes - we not only learn from our mistakes but it's where we find ideas.

Now you can use the plants with whatever technique you wish!

> ### HANDY TIP
>
> If you leave dried plant fibre on the lawn overnight the dew will moisten the fibres enough for use. In the morning while still damp, wrap the plant fibre with a wet towel while working. Fibres that are very thick will still need to be soaked.

NEW ZEALAND FLAX

NZ Flax, *Phormium tenax*, is native to New Zealand and traditionally used by Maori people to weave and make kete (baskets) as well as traditional ceremonial clothing. This is another favourite plant of basketmakers around the world.

It is a very strong and fibrous plant with long strappy leaves that can be split and woven.

This fibre is very versatile; you can pick and strip with a needle to the required width and use within a day or two. Otherwise you can pick, strip and bundle into coils, hang to dry and use when required. When you are ready to use the stripped fibres simply soak in water for five to ten minutes.

The plant comes in a variety of colours but will always dry to the same light brown. It is a pleasure to see the fibres change colour as they dry out.

The fibres can be used for coiling, twining, cordage and even stitching. This means you can make a whole piece with NZ Flax.

NZ Flax will tolerate frost, so good for the UK, Europe and parts of the US, but it does not like the tropics.

Opposite page:
Flax fibres
Photo by Ruth Woods

New Zealand Flax plant
Photo by Ruth Woods

This page:
Various pieces by Ruth Woods
Photo by Ruth Woods
Fibres: NZ Flax

BANANA FIBRE

Banana, *Musa sp.*, fibre is another basketmakers favourite and you may think this plant only grows in tropical places but it will grow in cooler countries like the UK. Grown for its enormous leaves rather than the fruit, it's the trunk that can be used for fibre to create basketry work and with a bit of care you can have a few plants in your garden.

Harvesting and Processing Banana for Basketry

by Helle Jorgensen

Banana is a herbaceous perennial which grows from a rhizome. The stem (pseudostem) is a tightly packed mass of overlapping and spirally arranged leaf sheaths.

Banana fibre is extremely fibrous and strong. It can be made into string, then looped, coiled or woven. In Japan it is made into cloth.

- After the plant has fruited, cut the stem down using a pruning saw or machete and remove the leaves.

- Separate as many of the overlapping leaf sheaths as possible using fingers. The inner sheaths can be difficult to separate, so you can leave those.

- Cut the sheaths longitudinally to the desired width using a sharp knife, typically a width of approximately 2 cm.

- Leave to dry in the sun. This may take several days depending on the climate. You can put them under cover overnight and then put them back out in the sun the following day. You can also leave them in a dry airy place such as garage or shed to dry.

- The material shrinks substantially because it initially contains a lot of water. Make sure you store your fibre in a dry airy space, this way it will last longer and not become mouldy. Once dry, it will only need a few minutes of soaking before ready to use.

- The inside part of the individual leaf sheath is considered by many as waste and can also be removed with a knife if desired. You can use both.

- Be aware that the sap can stain clothing permanently.

This page:
1. Banana plant, 2. Trunk cross-section, 3. Stem, 4. Leaf sheathes, 5. Leaves, 6. Regrowth, 7. Cut sheathes, 8. Banana fibre, 9. Knotless net
Photos by Helle Jorgenson

PALM TREES

Basketmakers always get excited when they find a palm inflorescence- the flower bearing stem, that has fallen from the tree as they are ideal for their creations. Inflorescence come in all shapes and sizes and there are other elements to be enjoyed from palm trees.

There are over two thousand species of palms throughout the world and pieces from palms have been incorporated in basketry for centuries. We will cover two types of palms The Date Palm *Phoenix sp.* and a palm with a crownshaft.

Palms with a crownshaft

Palms with a crownshaft are popular to use by basketmakers as there are several elements that can be incorporated. Species with a crownshaft include the Piccobeen Palm also known as a Bangalow Palm, *Archontophoenix cunninghamiana*, Alexander Palm, *Archontophoenix alexandrae* and Foxtail Palm, *Wodyetia bifurcata* to name a few.

The parts that can be incorporated are the inflorescence, the spathe also known as the bract - which houses the inflorescence and the sheathing base - while on the tree it is called a crownshaft and once it has fallen to the ground is known as the shealthing base.

Opposite page, clockwise from top left:

1. A Bangalow Palm crownshaft. Once this has fallen from the tree is known as the sheathing base and is attached to the frond (leaf). It turns a beautiful golden brown and will need to be sawn off from the frond as it is very hard. Soaking for several hours will make it flexible, and then can be cut and moulded to form a shape.

2. On the left - a sheathing base ready to be used. Many people find them so attractive they use them as a receptacle to display other items. Right - A Bangalow Palm spathe. These spathes are silky and soft and can be cut into strips and used in all types of weaving.

3. A container made from shaping a sheathing base from a Bangalow Palm.

4. An example of a large inflorescence hanging from a Bangalow Palm. Once it has dropped from the tree can be used straightaway as it will have dried. A quick soak in water will allow it to be pliable. The branchlets can be trimmed off and used in a woven, random weave or coiling technique.

Photos by Ruth Woods

Various Inflorescence
Photo by Ruth Woods

Date Palms

Date Palms, *Phoenix sp.*, is a genus of fourteen species of palms which grow all over the world. They have a completely different structure to an Alexander Palm and generally have a single trunk with no crown shaft and the inflorescence forms from a central point at the top of the trunk within a hard spathe.

The length of inflorescence will vary from 20 cm to 1.5 meters. All of the inflorescence are useful but the longer stems are the most desirable for making. The Canary Island Date Palms, *Phoenix dactylifera*, are featured in many botanical and public gardens around the world as they are a tall impressive palm. They can also tolerate heat, frost and very dry conditions. Because they are featured in many gardens you will often find fallen inflorescence, so being friends with the gardener and asking them to save these precious pieces could be a real bonus for your collection.

Using Date Palm inflorescence

Date Palm inflorescence branchlets can be trimmed from the central core and used in all types of basketry including coiling, weaving and random weave. To use, soak for a few minutes until pliable.

This page:
Top - **Date Palm inflorescence**
Bottom - **Date Palm inflorescence bundle**
Photos by Ruth Woods

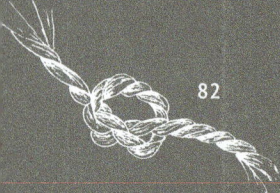

Date Palm
Phoenix sp.

Leaf or frond

Opening spathe

Inflorescence

VINES & CREEPERS

Vines are ideal for basketry projects. They can be used for all techniques and for both spokes and weavers and excellent for random weave. Some vines have a thick woody stem with appealing texture and others will be smooth with knotty nodes. Others, like grapevines and ivy have interesting tendrils which will add character to a piece.

Vines can be used for most techniques and really lends itself to explore the possibilities of sculptural pieces.

Some vines are considered invasive weeds like the Cat's Claw Creeper which has damaged many parts of NSW and Queensland. Gardeners and landcare groups are struggling to contain it. Then there are basketmakers who will happily go and help strip the invasive vine from the native trees and take home lots of material.

The Kudzu vine which is native to Asia is a hugely invasive plant and affecting many countries such as America, Japan and northern Australia. It can grow rapidly up to 30 metres long and can grow 30 cm a day! This vine can also be used for basketry, however when using it the waste must be disposed of carefully as it will take root wherever it lands.

Some vines are poisonous like the name suggests; Poisonous Ivy can cause bad irritations and dermatitis - so don't use it. The Common Ivy can be an irritant to some people so you might just wear gloves. But do your research first to make sure that the vine in your garden or park is safe to use.

Generally vines will need pruning, so check out your neighbour's garden and talk to the gardeners in the local parks; find out when they are pruning and ask if you can have the cuttings.

You can pick vines green or dry. Try and select long runners as they are good to work with. Roll them up into approximately 30 cm bundles. If they are green, let them dry out (they will shrink a lot). Rolling them onto bundles creates a memory in the stem and makes it easier to manipulate the vine with minimal cracking.

You will need to soak in water before use. How long you soak them will depend on the thickness of the vine. Fine vines can be wrapped in a wet towel; the thicker vines might need soaking for a few hours or overnight in a tub or bath until they are flexible.

Vines include - but are not limited to:

- Common Ivy - *Hedera helix*, **top right**
- Grapevines - *Vitis vinifera*
- Honeysuckle - *Loniceera sp.*, **bottom left**
- Passionfruit - *Passiflora edulis*
- Jasmine - *Jasminum sp.*
- Cat's Claw Creeper - *Dolichandra unguis-cati*
- Kiwi - *Actinidia chinensis*
- Coral Pea - *Hardenbergia violacea*
- Virginia Creeper - *Parthenocissus quinquefolia*
- Boston Ivy - *Parthenocissus tricuspidata*
- Lignum - *Muehlenbeckia sp.*
- Wisteria - *Wisteria sp.*
- Wonga Wonga Vine - *Pandorea pandorana*, **bottom right**
- Clematis - *Clematis sp.*
- Kudzu - *Pueraria sp.*

Daylily
Hemerocallis sp.

Bugle Lily, Watsonia
Watsonia

COMMON NAME · Daylily

BOTANICAL NAME · *Hemerocallis sp.*

FAMILY · *Asphodelaceae*

GROWN · These will grow in most climates, are drought tolerant and need little maintenance.

BASKETRY INFORMATION · A lovely fibre that is soft and supple. It is excellent for cordage, which can then be coiled or used in twined baskets.

HOW TO HARVEST · Can be picked green, or look for leaves that are already brown and have fallen between the green leaves; these can be used straight away.

HOW TO DRY · If you pick green leaves, dry them by spreading them out on a flat surface and allow to dry a yellow / brown colour.

HOW TO USE · Only re-hydrate what you think you will use; it is easy to prepare more. Wrap up the plant fibre in a wet towel and they should be ready to use in about 20 minutes.

COMMON NAME · Bugle Lily, Watsonia

BOTANICAL NAME · *Watsonia sp.*

FAMILY · *Iridaceae*

GROWN · Native to South Africa, commonly grown in temperate areas.

BASKETRY INFORMATION · This soft long leafy plant has a core down the centre and dries a dark golden colour. Can be used for all types of basketry.

HOW TO HARVEST · Pick leaves at base of the plant after flowering in early spring.

HOW TO DRY · Hang in small bunches upside down in a dry airy place.

HOW TO USE · Soak in warm water until pliable and wrapped in a damp towel.

Red Hot Poker
Kniphofia sp.

Lomandra or Mat-Rush
Lomandra sp.

COMMON NAME · Red Hot Poker

BOTANICAL NAME · *Kniphofia sp.*

FAMILY · *Asphodelaceae*

GROWN · South African species tolerate cool-temperate climates and will grow in the UK and southern Australia. Species from tropical and sub-tropical Africa need a milder climate and will not tolerate frost. All need good drainage.

BASKETRY INFORMATION · A much-loved basketry fibre in Australia. This is a soft fibre and a joy to work with. It dries a pinky beige colour and is excellent for all types of basketry.

HOW TO HARVEST · Cut at base when green.

HOW TO DRY · Bundle in small bunches of approximately 6 - 8 leaves with an elastic band, and hang until dry in an airy place. This can take a couple of weeks or a month or two, depending on the weather.

HOW TO USE · Soak for about 15 minutes or until pliable. Wrap in a damp towel while using.

COMMON NAME · Lomandra or Mat-Rush

BOTANICAL NAME · *Lomandra sp.*; there are more than 50 species native to Australasia

FAMILY · *Asparagaceae*

GROWN · This tough plant is common in all climates.

BASKETRY INFORMATION · Easy to use and readily available in lots of gardens. Can be used for coiling, twining, random weave and stitching.

HOW TO HARVEST · Cut outer leaves as near to base as possible. The flowers are prickly so be careful when picking. The dried plant will shrink but can be used fresh for 1 - 7 days.

HOW TO DRY · Split into fine lengths approximately 2 - 4 mm wide. Leave in a cool, dry place. Can be bundled and hung or left on a bench to dry.

HOW TO USE · Use fresh for a few days. If left to dry, soak for about 15 minutes then wrap in a damp towel.

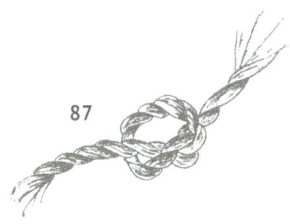

Madagascar Dragon Tree
Dracaena marginata

Dragon Tree
Dracaena draco

COMMON NAME · Madagascar Dragon Tree

BOTANICAL NAME · *Dracaena reflexa var. angustifolia, syn. Dracaena marginata*

FAMILY · *Asparagaceae*

GROWN · Warm, sub tropical and tropical areas. Popular as house plants.

BASKETRY INFORMATION · Common indoor and outdoor plant. Also comes in variegated forms. Can be used for cordage, coiling, could be used for weaving but leaves are relatively short - 20 - 30 cm.

HOW TO HARVEST · As new leaves grow, old leaves turn yellow and drop. You can pick yellowing leaves directly from the plant or ground.

HOW TO DRY · The leaves usually fall off the plant dry or semi dry. Lay flat in an airy place until they dry completely.

HOW TO USE · Moisten by wrapping in a damp towel or soak in warm water until pliable.

COMMON NAME · Dragon Tree

BOTANICAL NAME · *Dracaena draco*

FAMILY · *Asparagaceae*

GROWN · Thrives in a hot, dry climate but also found in tropical and subtropical areas.

BASKETRY INFORMATION · Basketmakers love this plant as the sheathing base is bright orange and is a real feature in any basket.

HOW TO HARVEST · Gather leaves that have fallen, as they are dry and ready to use after soaking.

HOW TO DRY · Usually already dry when gathering.

HOW TO USE · Soak for an hour or so until pliable.

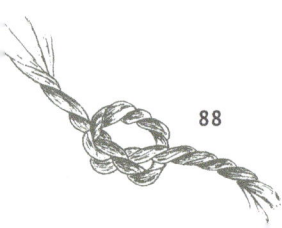

Arum Lily
Zantedeschia aethiopica

New Zealand Flax or Harakeke
Phormium tenax

COMMON NAME · Arum Lily

BOTANICAL NAME · *Zantedeschia aethiopica*

FAMILY · *Araceae*

GROWN · Grows in moist areas; evergreen in warm, wet climate but will die back if there is a dry season, regrowing in wetter months. Native to Africa but an invasive weed in many cool-temperate climates.

BASKETRY INFORMATION · You can use both the flower and leaf stem. This is a soft fibre to work with. Good for cordage, coiling, twining. Can be used with the whole stem or split into finer strips.

HOW TO HARVEST · Cut when green or as the stalk begins to yellow and die back.

HOW TO DRY · Bundle about four stems with an elastic band at base of stem. They take several months to dry, will shrink enormously and need to be re-bundled.

HOW TO USE · A quick run under the tap or wrap in a wet towel. Be careful not to oversoak as it will become too wet to use.

COMMON NAME · New Zealand Flax / Harakeke

BOTANICAL NAME · *Phormium tenax*

FAMILY · *Asphodelaceae*

GROWN · Generally cool-temperate climates - Native to New Zealand.

BASKETRY INFORMATION · A favourite of basketmakers and known for the traditional Maori baskets. Can be used for coiling, stitching, twining and other basketry techniques.

HOW TO HARVEST · Cut outer leaves at base of plant. Can be split and used straight away or split and bundled into a coils and used later.

HOW TO DRY · Split to required width from 1 mm up to 1 cm wide and coil into bundles.

HOW TO USE · Use fresh or can be split then dried. If dried then wrap in a damp towel until fibre is flexible.

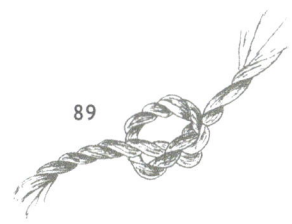

Cordyline / Cabbage Tree
Cordyline australis

Yucca
Yucca filamentosa

COMMON NAME · Cordyline / Cabbage Tree

BOTANICAL NAME · *Cordyline australis*

FAMILY · *Asparagaceae*

GROWN · Although native to warm-temperate New Zealand, this Cordyline species is tough and will grow in most climates.

BASKETRY INFORMATION · Leaves are quite firm so are often used for spokes in a woven or twined basket.

HOW TO HARVEST · Fallen leaves can be gathered.

HOW TO DRY · Usually already dry when leaves have dropped - otherwise dry in an airy place.

HOW TO USE · Soak for an hour or until the leaves become pliable.

COMMON NAME · Yucca

BOTANICAL NAME · *Yucca filamentosa*

FAMILY · *Asparagaceae*

GROWN · Generally prefers dryer, warmer climates but has adapted to a range of climates.

BASKETRY INFORMATION · There are many species of Yucca and most are suitable for basketry. Taking care with the spiky ends, the long strappy leaves can be used for many basketry techniques. Tough enough to use as basket stakes and makes strong cordage for handles.

HOW TO HARVEST · Leaves that are already brown on the plant can be collected and used immediately. Green leaves can be picked and dried.

HOW TO DRY · Individual leaves can be dried whole in airy place or can be split using a needle first. Leaves can also be tied in a small bundles and dried.

HOW TO USE · Re-hydrate by soaking for 10 minutes or until pliable.

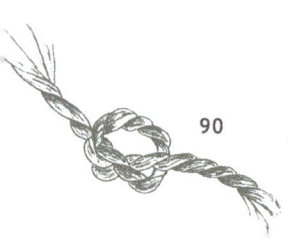

Cordyline / Slender Palm Lily
Cordyline stricta

Daffodil, Narcissus, Jonquil
Narcissus sp.

COMMON NAME · Cordyline / Slender Palm Lily

BOTANICAL NAME · *Cordyline stricta*

FAMILY · *Asparagaceae*

GROWN · Although found in warm-temperate and sub-tropical Australia, it is quite a resilient plant and will grow in most climates.

BASKETRY INFORMATION · Leaves are softer than *Cordyline australis*. The feature of this leaf is that it will turn a very dark colour if dried in direct sunlight. This can give a basket a good colour contrast. Can be used for coiling, twining and cordage.

HOW TO HARVEST · Leaves can be picked at the base of a branch.

HOW TO DRY · Try to dry in sunlight. Hot sun will give a dark colour. It can then be bundled into small bunches and allowed to fully dry.

HOW TO USE · Soak for a few hours or until it becomes pliable.

COMMON NAME · Daffodil, Narcissus, Jonquil

BOTANICAL NAME · *Narcissus sp.*

FAMILY · *Amaryllidaceae*

GROWN · Native to Europe, Africa and Asia, and now grown worldwide.

BASKETRY INFORMATION · This is soft fibre to work with and excellent for cordage, which can then be coiled, or twined into a basket.

HOW TO HARVEST · If you tie up your Daffodils, wait for them to dry out before picking. Otherwise pick leaves once they have wilted.

HOW TO DRY · Tie in small bunches and store in a dry place or lay flat on a table. When dry, wrap in newspaper and store.

HOW TO USE · Wrap in a damp towel until fibres are pliable. This should only take 10 minutes or so. Or run under a tap for a minute. Keep wrapped in the damp towel, as they will dry out quickly.

Tulip
Tulipa sp.

Iris
Iris sp.

COMMON NAME · Tulip

BOTANICAL NAME · *Tulipa sp.*

FAMILY · *Liliaceae*

GROWN · Worldwide; bulbs must be lifted and chilled in warmer climates.

BASKETRY INFORMATION · This is a soft fibre to work with and excellent for cordage, which can then be coiled or twined into a basket.

HOW TO HARVEST · If you prefer to tie up your tulips leaves, wait for them to dry before picking. Otherwise pick leaves once they have wilted.

HOW TO DRY · Tie in small bundles and store in a dry place or lay flat on a table. When dry, wrap in newspaper and store.

HOW TO USE · Wrap in a damp towel until fibres are pliable. This should only take 10 minutes. Or run under a tap for a minute. Keep wrapped in the damp towel as they will dry out quickly.

COMMON NAME · Iris

BOTANICAL NAME · *Iris sp.*

FAMILY · *Iridaceae*

GROWN · Worldwide: Europe, Americas, Asia, Africa, and Australasia.

BASKETRY INFORMATION · All types of Iris can be incorporated into basketry. It is very fibrous, makes strong cordage and can be used for all techniques.

HOW TO HARVEST · Cut green, or pull yellow leaves gently from the plant.

HOW TO DRY · Bundle into small bunches and hang to dry; they will take a month or so as their leaves are quite thick.

HOW TO USE · Wrap in a damp towel for 15 minutes or so. Keep wrapped in a damp towel while using.

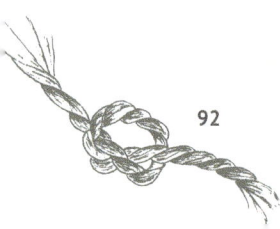

Kangaroo Paw
Anigozanthos sp.,

Bulrush / Cumbungi / Reedmace / Cattail / Raupo
Typha sp.

COMMON NAME · Kangaroo Paw

BOTANICAL NAME · *Anigozanthos sp.*

FAMILY · *Haemodoraceae*

GROWN · Native to Western Australia. Increasingly sold in USA and Europe.

BASKETRY INFORMATION · Can be used for coiling and weaving.

HOW TO HARVEST · Pick at base of plants. Avoid the fur on flower stalks, as it can irritate skin and eyes on contact.

HOW TO DRY · Bundle into small bunches and hang to dry.

HOW TO USE · Can be used for string and incorporated into coiling.

COMMON NAME · Bulrush / Cumbungi / Reedmace / Cattail / Raupo

BOTANICAL NAME · *Typha sp.*

FAMILY · *Typhaceae*

GROWN · Worldwide.

BASKETRY INFORMATION · This is probably the most common plant used for basketry around the world, which is why it has so many different names. It is a versatile plant that can be used in all areas of basketry.

HOW TO HARVEST · Pick when green and, if possible, before flowering.

HOW TO DRY · Create small bundles, tie at one end and hang in a dry, airy place.

HOW TO USE · Wrap in damp towels for an hour or soak for 10 minutes until the plant is pliable. Can be used for all techniques in basketry.

Lavender
Lavandula sp.

Corn / Maize
Zea mays

COMMON NAME · Lavender

BOTANICAL NAME · *Lavandula sp.*

FAMILY · *Lamiaceae*

GROWN · World wide; can be grown in all climates but will need more care in the tropics.

BASKETRY INFORMATION · Incorporate lavender into a basket for its flower and its scent. Can be used in a coiled basket.

HOW TO HARVEST · Pick when flowering.

HOW TO DRY · Hang to dry in a dry, airy place.

HOW TO USE · If using dried lavender, moisten the stalks so they become flexible; fresh lavender should have enough flexibility to be coiled.

COMMON NAME · Corn / Maize

BOTANICAL NAME · *Zea mays*

FAMILY · *Poaceae*

GROWN · Worldwide; can be grown in most climates.

BASKETRY INFORMATION · Use the outside sheath of the corn cob, which can be obtained from the plant or supermarket! Ask the staff at the shop if they have any in store from cobs that have been put on display. Even though the sheaths are quite short, they are strong and flexible; the pale colour adds another contrast.

HOW TO HARVEST · Take the sheath off the cob when the cob has been picked or buy from your supermarket. Eat the corn and save the sheath!

HOW TO DRY · Already dry; store in a dry place.

HOW TO USE · Give a quick spray with water from a spray bottle; this should be enough to soften so it can be manipulated to incorporate into a coiled basket.

Philodendron Selloum
Thaumatophyllum bipinnatifidum

Gymea Lily
Doryanthes excelsa

COMMON NAME · Philodendron Selloum

BOTANICAL NAME · *Thaumatophyllum bipinnatifidum syn. Philodendron bipinnatifidum*

FAMILY · *Araceae*

GROWN · Tropical, sub-tropical and warm-temperate climates but grown worldwide as a house plant.

BASKETRY INFORMATION · A large-leafed plant. The sheath of the leaf is used; it is a honey colour once dried and does not change. It is soft, flexible and can be used in all areas of basketry.

HOW TO HARVEST · Look to the central trunk of the plant and you'll see the large, drying brown sheaths; gently pick (they could still be connected to the plant, only remove once the leaf has emerged.

HOW TO DRY · They are ready to use.

HOW TO USE · You can use straight away if still pliable. If they have dried out, wrap up in a damp towel or immerse in water for ten minutes or until pliable.

COMMON NAME · Gymea Lily

BOTANICAL NAME · *Doryanthes excelsa*

FAMILY · *Doryanthaceae*

GROWN · Native to coastal New South Wales but widely used in landscaping; available online overseas.

BASKETRY INFORMATION · The leaves can be used for coiling, cordage and weaving.

HOW TO HARVEST · Cut outer leaves and split.

HOW TO DRY · Pick green leaves from the base of the plant; they can take many months to dry. Take out the middle rib, discard and roll the rest into a coil. Leaves turn a golden-brown colour.

HOW TO USE · Soak dried leaves overnight then wrap in a damp towel.

Foxtail Agave
Agave attenuata

Jacaranda
Jacaranda mimosifolia

COMMON NAME · Foxtail Agave

BOTANICAL NAME · *Agave attenuata*

FAMILY · *Asparagaceae*

GROWN · Native to Mexico; will grow in temperate, subtropical and tropical areas.

BASKETRY INFORMATION · A thick, strong leaf. Good for cordage and handles. Can be cut into strips for finer cordage.

HOW TO HARVEST · If you can find plants under cover in a pot they are usually cleaner. Pick leaves from the base of the plants that are already dry to keep the sheath intact (this is where the leaf attaches to the main stem). Fresh leaves will take many months to dry, up to a year!

HOW TO DRY · Already dried when picked, or leave on a sunny windowsill and wait!

HOW TO USE · Soak until pliable; wrap in a damp towel to keep moist while using.

COMMON NAME · Jacaranda

BOTANICAL NAME · *Jacaranda mimosifolia*

FAMILY · *Bignoniaceae*

GROWN · A tree native to South America, commonly grown in temperate and subtropical areas.

BASKETRY INFORMATION · Jacaranda leaf stalks are used in basketry. The beautiful golden-brown, fine twigs are ideal for coiling - similar to using pine needles.

HOW TO HARVEST · Easy to gather when the leaves fall in autumn.

HOW TO DRY · Leave on a bench until dry - many will already be dry when collected and ready to use. Can be stored in a ventilated box.

HOW TO USE · Soak in warm water for 30 minutes and wrapped in a damp towel.

Sheoak
Casuarina and Allocasuarina

African Flag
Chasmanthe floribunda

COMMON NAME · Sheoak

BOTANICAL NAME · *Casuarina sp. & Allocasuarina sp.* - there are more than 60 species of Allocasuarina in Australia plus 14 species of Casuarina across a wider range.

FAMILY · *Casuarinaceae*

GROWN · Native to Australia, Pacific, Asia and Africa. Will grow in cooler and warmer climates.

BASKETRY INFORMATION · This evergreen tree has thin, scaley, pine-like foliage. The male flowers form golden-brown catkin-like ends to the branchlets. Some species have especially long foliage, which can be used to incorporate into the core.

HOW TO HARVEST · Prune branches off trees

HOW TO DRY · Can be used straight away or dried for later use.

HOW TO USE · Can be dried for later use.

COMMON NAME · African Flag

BOTANICAL NAME · *Chasmanthe floribunda*

FAMILY · *Iridaceae*

GROWN · Native to South Africa, commonly grown in temperate areas.

BASKETRY INFORMATION · This soft long leafy plant dries a pale golden colour. It's usually preferred by basketmakers over Watsonia as it is softer and more pliable and has no core in the leaf. It can be used for all types of basketry and also has a very decorative bulb that can be incorporated into pieces.

HOW TO HARVEST · Pick leaves at the base of the plant after flowering in early spring. You can also incorporate the top of the bulb which will often come away with leaves when picking.

HOW TO DRY · Hang in small bunches upside down in a dry airy place.

HOW TO USE · Soak in warm water until pliable and wrapped in a damp towel.

Tall Spike-Rush
Eleocharis sphacelata

Tussock Grasses
Poa sp.

COMMON NAME · Tall Spike-Rush

BOTANICAL NAME · *Eleocharis sphacelata*

FAMILY · *Cyperaceae*

GROWN · Found in wetlands across much of Australasia

BASKETRY INFORMATION · A long, hollow-stemmed rush 1.5 metres to 2 metres tall, which can be as thick as a little finger. It can be split finer or used whole. It is good for all techniques in basketmaking, and in particular weaving around spokes.

HOW TO HARVEST · Cut at base of plant. This can be a little hard if the plant is submerged in water. Cutting in summer is good, when water levels are usually lower and the outer reeds can be reached.

HOW TO DRY · Lay flat in a dry place; shuffle reeds around to allow air access. Can be bundled into a hammock-type structure.

HOW TO USE · Wrap in a damp towel for 15 minutes or so. Keep wrapped in a damp towel while using.

COMMON NAME · Tussock Grasses, many types of grass can be used

BOTANICAL NAME · *Poa sp.*

FAMILY · *Poaceae*

GROWN · Native to Australia, Pacific, Asia and Africa. Will grow in cooler and warmer climates.

BASKETRY INFORMATION · These grasses can be found all over the globe, often in pastures, and are popular for ornamental use in gardens. Use what's available. Good for coiling and as a bulk fibre.

HOW TO HARVEST · Cut when the grass looks dry.

HOW TO DRY · Pick when dry; it will be ready for immediate use.

HOW TO USE · Poa grasses are pliable enough to use when dry; if using another species, look for grasses that are fine and flexible. Incorporate small bundles into the core of a coiled basket.

OTHER MATERIALS

RAFFIA

What is Raffia?

Raffia is a natural fibre that is perfect for basket weaving; it is strong, easily malleable and kind to your hands. Basketmakers use raffia for its ease of use and aesthetic qualities. Once woven together, raffia can produce a good-looking product and if you're a beginner, it's very forgiving.

The term raffia often gets used to describe anything that resembles raffia - like a flat or papery type yarn, such as paper, bamboo, viscose or cellophane raffia; these are also useful weaving materials, but tend to be continuous, softer and potentially paper, synthetic or plastic.

In this book when we refer to raffia, we are talking specifically about the species of palm tree native to Madagascar, usually *Raphia taedigera*. This fibre is biodegradable and has had no chemical treatment.

This page, top to bottom:
Kilo hanks of raffia stored in a Madagascan warehouse, A Raffia Palm
Photo by Komel Hirdjee

Opposite page:
One kilo hank of raffia

The history of raffia harvesting for fibre is long and is a fundamental part of the material culture of the Malagasy people of Madagascar and is integral to the production of Malagasy raffia cloth as a trade commodity for over 1400 years.

These days, raffia is an important export fibre for Madagascar and has become a popular fibre for basket weaving, particularly in Australia.

On a palm tree, the 'leaf' is actually what we might think of as a 'whole branch', so the leaves on the raffia palm are commonly over 15 metres long and up to 3 or 4 metres wide. The segments are the dried and shredded 'leafy bits' becoming the raffia fibre we use.

For the export market, raffia is graded and sorted by quality. There are many different grades used, but the popular grades for weaving tend to be known as florist grade (for their longest length, over 1.5 metres) and superior (1.2 - 1.5 metres). Raffia is bundled tightly at the top, and bound in a characteristic tie. These are referred to as hanks, and hanks typically weigh around 1 kg.

Raffia from similar palms from elsewhere, such as Indonesia or Philippines may appear similar at first, but tends to be more brittle, softer and shorter in length and not as pleasant to use.

Dyed Raffia

Dyes suitable for cotton and wool will also work on raffia. Generally speaking, raffia takes dyes quite easily but it's important to remember the base is a warm beige, not a white, which means results will differ from what you might expect with wool or cotton. If you use natural dyes, this will require quite a lot of experimenting to see what will work as it is very different to dyeing other fibres with a natural dyeing process.

Using Raffia

Raffia is an excellent fibre to use for coiling, stitching, crochet, as well as loom weaving. As it is so strong and yet pliable, it is no surprise it is popular as a basket and sculptural weaving material. It is used throughout the world to make hats, bags, baskets, rugs, woven fabrics, shoes and interior furnishings.

Remember that raffia is a natural fibre that is processed by humans, not a machine, and therefore, there will be inconsistencies in the strand lengths and thicknesses.

If you examine a strand of raffia you'll notice one end that is thin and more woody and the other flat, wider, soft and maybe split.

Raffia can be worked as it comes and have a natural tendency to split. As you work through your bundle, you will be left with many finer strands. Keep these as they are very handy to make cordage, to stitch with or use in the core.

by Cass Harris - String Harvest

RECYCLED MATERIALS

Recycled materials - Search your Stash

In this age of mass consumption and waste, using recycled materials is a way to support the planet and reduce your own footprint. In Australia it's estimated that 6000 kg of textile waste goes to landfill every ten minutes (ABC, War on Waste).

Crafters often have their own accumulation of materials and fabrics at the ready – and there's just something so satisfying about breathing new life into old materials. Those that don't have their own stockpile of things to use, can search in charity shops (op shops and thrift stores), even asking friends and family for good quality throw-outs. It's easy to gather an array of interesting materials very quickly.

Recycled Fabrics

Fabrics are ideal for creating basketry vessels using various techniques. If you're a sewer, you can use most clothing materials, fabric from a half-finished project or dive into your craft stash that has been growing for years.

When visiting charity shops, look for the bargain rack or things on sale as you will often find items suitable to cut up for making. Look at colours that inspire you and use fabrics that feel good to touch - natural fibres, linen, cotton, wool and silk are all good to use.

Denim is a fantastic material to include and jeans are a great basketry resource. You can use almost the whole garment; the fabric cut into strips, the seams, pockets, and waistband. Most households have a pair or two that are on their last legs or have gone out of fashion and are lying in a cupboard somewhere.

Ropes and cord

There is no limit on what cords you can use in basketry, many of which can be recycled. Rope is left behind on building sites, telephone installations and on the beach.

Ropes can often be found in your garage; have a good search and see what you can find - making sure it's not allocated for some other use!

There are many other types of cord and rope that can be incorporated into basketry such as baling twine which is usually blue, but you might also come across pink and yellow. It is great to use in the core of a textile coiled basket where it can be hidden completely or left exposed to take advantage of the colour.

There are several fibre artists who use ghost nets (discarded fishing nets and marine rope). These nets are a little harder to find but there will be areas along some coastlines that collect more rubbish than others due to the tides.

Discarded fishing material is a huge environmental problem for our oceans, so the more you find the better! After gathering rope and netting, you will need to clean and sort them ready for making. It is also advisable to wear a mask when using these materials as they can have degraded somewhat.

105

Plastics

Plastic bags can be made into surprisingly strong cordage. Vegetable bags, bread wrappers and carrier bags can all be used in many techniques.

Threads

There is an array of threads that can be sourced either by picking up when scouring thrift shops, craft shops or online stores. Don't forget to look in your craft stash for wool, embroidery threads and even string.

Generally, natural threads are ideal for basketry work. Linens, cotton, wool, hemp, and jute all work well. Waxed threads are even better but can be costly if your budget is an issue. You can easily create your own by using a block of beeswax and pulling a length of thread through the beeswax to create a coating. This then makes a great fibre to stitch with that helps to keep the stitches in place.

Wire

Wire can be stripped from old electrical cables and used in basketry. You'd also be amazed at how much is sitting around in people's garages! If you know an electrician you could be in luck as they might be able to give you an unlimited supply.

Opposite page:
A Drop in the Ocean by Carolyn Cardinet
Photo by Carolyn Cardinet
Fibres: Baling twine

Artist's statement:
A Drop in the Ocean is a compelling vibrant blue sculptural piece made from plastic baling twine collected, saved and transformed to create awareness of the daily plastic waste that reaches and pollutes waterways and oceans.
Be the change .... We are earth, we are air, we are water.

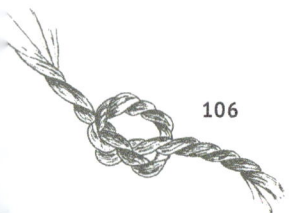

MAKING WAX THREAD

As well as using plant fibre or recycled materials to create sculptural basketry, you could find the need to use commercial thread for assembling and joining structures, weaving or looping.

One of the most handy threads to have in your collection is waxed linen thread or artificial sinews. These are not always easy to buy unless you belong to a basketry group. However you can make your own waxed thread by taking linen or cotton thread, cutting a length about one metre (forty inches) and pulling the thread through a block of beeswax a few times until you can feel the waxy coating on the thread. You can usually buy beeswax from a market stall that sells local honey. Making your own thread saves a lot of money as waxed linen thread is very expensive.

THREE ARTISTS USING RECYCLED MATERIALS

This page:
Kooky Tree
Photo by the artist
Fibres: recycled clothing, cardboard and raffia

See more of Fleur's work on page 22

Fleur Brett

One of the major materials Fleur works with in her sculpture is industrial data cable. She first discovered this as a medium to use when the owner of a salvage yard gave her some cable offcuts in different sizes to experiment with. When Fleur worked out which size was suitable, she was able to purchase the cable by weight which was quite cheap. She has created several sculptures using a random weave technique and giant French knitting. She also unwinds old work and weaves with this reclaimed cable to create new installations.

Jess Lietmanis

In Jess's woven sculptural pieces she predominantly works with marine debris rope and has travelled on numerous beach clean-up trips with various environmental organisations and retrieved rope from remote coastlines of Australia. Much of this material has come from the Southwest National Park in Tasmania, a Wilderness World Heritage Area. She also has rope from the opposite end of the country, the coastline of Kutini-Payamu National Park in Cape York.

Most of the rope she works with is severely faded and perished, so she'll unravel the fibres to expose this variation of hue and texture. When unraveling degraded rope—a process that causes high friction and often dislodges micro plastic, Jess is diligent in wearing a mask to prevent inhalation of this inorganic material. The fibre processing can take up to 1/3 of the overall construction time.

This page:
Detail of Cocoon of Convenience 1200 B.C.E.
Photo by the artist
Fibres: Salvaged marine debris rope and fishing line

See more of Jess's work on page 30

This page:
Textile mats
Photo by Ruth Woods
Fibres: Recycled fabric offcuts

Ruth Woods

Ruth uses recycled fabrics from worn-out clothes or items she has purchased from charity shops. She loves to collect men's shirts as these have the best selection of colour. In her craft stash she has a large supply of jeans and is always on the lookout for a good pair of Levi's. She gets a great feeling when she is able to give these fabrics a new life. Creating textile coiled baskets is what she's known for and she has a large accumulation of fabrics in her studio ready to use in her next creation.

CREATE

In this section you are invited to explore and play with the fibres and techniques we cover in this book; to fully engage and lose yourself in this magical place of making.

If you have worked with basketry techniques before and want to explore a more intuitive and creative path, you have a head start on this journey.

If you're new to these techniques or just dabbled a little, you're at an advantage because you'll start from scratch with a fresh perspective. Either way you can produce some amazing creative work.

This section goes through several techniques; weaving, looping, coiling, random weave and cordage. All of these methods are practised worldwide. What makes them unique to certain countries are the fibres that are used.

When learning some of these basic techniques, be prepared to play, experiment, explore, research and document your thoughts. This is a creative process and not about producing finished pieces every time but making work that inspires you to delve deeper and push into unexplored areas for you. It's a valuable creative learning process; allow yourself time and keep that inner critic at bay.

Progress is more important than perfection; we can get so caught up about technique and trying to be perfect will hold you back from creating your art.

Like any new artwork or medium it can feel frustrating, scary and exciting. But we need to learn to trust the process and get into the 'Flow', when you do this you will experience the joy of making and realising some fabulous results.

TECHNIQUES

PRACTICE PROJECTS

All the techniques listed in this book can be used to create practice projects.

Part of the creative learning process and developing work is to allow yourself to go on a journey of gaining new skills, developing ideas and experimenting. By practising new skills and working with them for a period of time you will become familiar with how the techniques work and how you can use them differently. Using various materials also allows you to experiment and blend the techniques and fibres. Then you can experiment with shape - bringing them all together and expanding the scope of your work.

You can ask yourself: what happens if I do this; what happens if I use that? Don't be scared to try. There are no solid rules, only guidelines and tips and because you are the artist, you can play around and develop your ideas as you wish. Don't judge yourself - this is something we all do that can limit how we work and at times stop us working altogether. Treating the work as practice will allow your work to progress differently; the ideas will flow more easily - allow yourself time and you will be surprised at the results. It is said that Picasso drew hundreds of sketches before he embarked on his final paintings.

Accessing your flow state to try out and explore new ideas is certainly beneficial - however it can be frustrating when we feel we are not achieving what we want, understanding that this is normal and part of the artistic process is helpful for your development as an artist and to push your work and create new ideas.

In this book I talk about making Practice Projects as an approach to learning. It can be a real advantage to allow yourself to play in this manner.

Play is vital - it gives us approval to be ourselves, come up with crazy ideas without listening to the little voice in our head. We will not judge ourselves if we are just playing; we can stop and start, leave things unfinished, start new pieces, explore and document new ideas.

All you will need is a notebook and your fibre, maybe some thread and a needle. Then just start. In this process we are not trying to finish things; we are in the creative learning space and you have permission to be there. Keep all the things you make - even if you don't like them or they're unfinished; we are going to collect our Practice Projects later; consider them them as your think tank and a repository of ideas. This is why your notebook or journal is beneficial - document those ideas no matter how crazy they seem.

A wall of Practice Projects using many techniques and fibres.
Photo by Sean Paris

STARTING YOUR WORK

Some tips on how to begin

Keep a journal

Keeping a journal or a simple notebook is way of documenting what you do, where you find your plants or recycled materials and the techniques and the hundreds of ideas that come flowing in.

It is a tool that will help you develop concepts and your own style. If keeping a journal is something new to you - try it and once you start you'll understand its benefits.

Start small

Playing and experimenting with small pieces is a good way to obtain results easily and quickly. As you create you'll want to make more because you are achieving results. If you are new to these techniques and embark on a large piece of work, you could find it overwhelming and difficult; then you're more likely to be disappointed and not want to continue - keep it manageable to start. Hold on to the things you create.

Be curious

Continually look for new fibres, try new techniques and explore shape. Go for a walk in the forest, on the beach, look in a friends garden, drop into a Reverse Garbage store (a place that recycle really interesting materials). Inspiration can come from places we least expect.

Look for shapes within branches, bark, waste metal pieces and recycled objects. Think about how they might be used and how it might fit within your work. Don't discount small objects as these are good for practice.

Visit exhibitions

Exhibitions are a great way to open your eyes to new things but visiting exhibitions of basketmakers and basketry artists will limit your ideas. Of course they have their place but if you want to be innovative and different, also visit art exhibitions not related to your medium.

Biennale exhibitions, which are held around the world in larger cities every two years, are a tremendously rich source of inspiration. Search to see if there are any near you. If you can't visit them in person they often have excellent online access. Make it a habit to visit a variety of exhibitions.

Explore new techniques, materials and shape

Learn and experiment with new techniques because sometimes we make mistakes and we invent a new way of doing something. Create many samples with the same method using a variety of different materials. Also try using the same fibre with other techniques. Don't have any expectations, see what evolves. This can give you an abundance of options to work with.

Remember, progress is better than perfection.

This page:
A collection of Philodendron leaf sheaths turned into cordage
Photo by Sean Paris

Being original

As you develop your work, you will look at others to try and replicate them - this is part of learning. However it's good practice to acknowledge our teachers and inspirations.

Look at artists / sculptors that interest you, research them, find out what has influenced and inspired them. Examine artists that are outside your everyday scope of interest. You might find some new and interesting ideas that you can interpret with the materials you are using.

By delving into form, technique, materials and working with your practice pieces, you will push your ideas. As you continue on your creative journey, your work will expand and you will develop your own style.

Just start making!

WHEN CHOOSING TO CREATE; DON'T EVER BE AFRAID TO MAKE MISTAKES. WE NOT ONLY LEARN FROM THEM, BUT IT'S OFTEN WHERE WE FIND IDEAS.

Ruth Woods

Working on a vine structure starting to overlay with looping.
Photo by Sean Paris

TOOLS

With the techniques used in this book you need very few basic tools. You don't need to go and buy expensive equipment. Remember, basketry has been around for many centuries and basketmakers would have had very basic tools.

- A selection of needles with a large eye such as a darning or chenille needle
- A hook of some kind; a crochet hook or latch needle
- Sharp scissors
- A reasonably sharp knife to cut grass or rush. Tie a piece of string to the handle and wrap around your wrist. This is a good idea so you don't lose it in the water.
- Numerous clips, pegs or clamps to hold fibre in place.
- Tape to hold fibre in place.
- Strong thread - waxed linen thread or thread and beeswax to wax the thread.
- Secateurs - it's a good idea to have a couple of pairs and keep one pair in the car.
- Balls and small forms for moulding when making a fine random weave piece.
- A few cable ties - try not to overuse these as they are plastic. Use to start off the random weave shapes (thicker fibre) for the first few hoops and then use waxed thread.
- String and rubber bands to bundle your fibre

TECHNIQUES INDEX

CORDAGE
Page 126

BRAIDING
Page 128

COILING
Page 130

WEAVING
Page 140

LOOPING
Page 148

RANDOM WEAVE
Page 152

This page:
A collection of cordage using many different plant fibres
Photo by Sean Paris

Opposite page:
A coiled piece using cordage
Photo by Sean Paris

CORDAGE

Cordage is a valuable technique and extremely useful for incorporating into basketry.

It is made by twisting two strands of fibre together and can be used for weaving, coiling and is quite appealing on its own.

When you have an excess of suitable plant fibre you can create cordage and store until required. This technique can sometimes be a bit confusing to start with but when you have mastered this simple skill, you will love it as it is satisfying and addictive.

Fibre suggestions

Dried soft flexible fibres are recommended, for example, Daylily, Daffodils, Red Hot Poker, Iris, Banana, or you can use strips of material.

The fibre will need to be flexible, so it will be necessary to rehydrate dried leaves to twist without cracking. Depending on the fibre, soak for a few minutes in hot water until pliable. Don't oversoak, as the fibres will swell up and shrink when dried. Once the leaves are moist, keep in a damp towel while you are making the cord. Don't leave the fibre wrapped for more than a day or it will go mouldy.

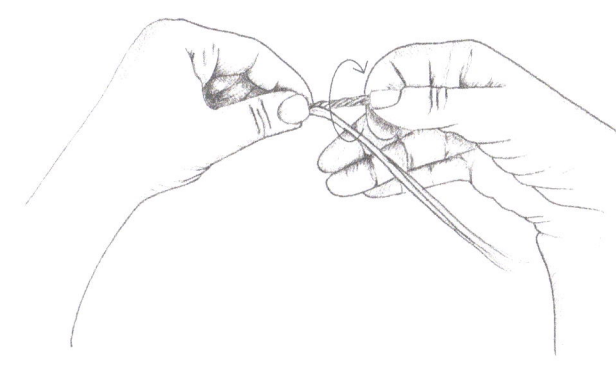

Making the cord

Tie two ends of the plant fibre together or fold one long piece in half, slightly off-centre.

Hold the ends of the fibre with your non-dominant hand, with the strands sticking out at right angle from your thumb and forefinger - so there is a top and a bottom strand.

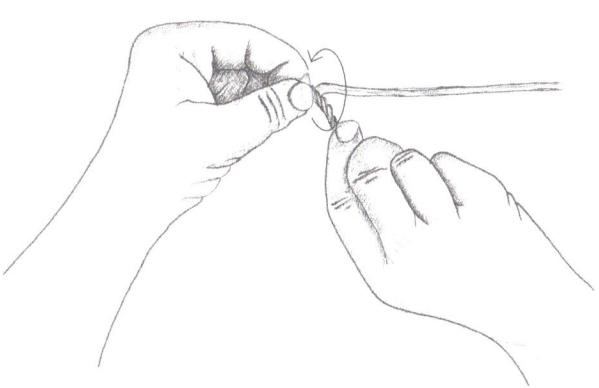

With your dominant hand, twist the top strand away from you, then bring forward over the top of the bottom strand so the two strands are swapping places.

Repeat, twisting the top strand away from you and then bringing it over the top of the bottom strand.

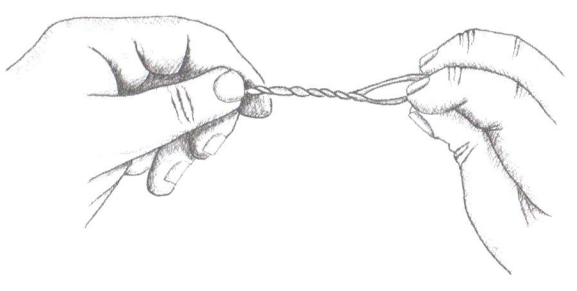

Move your non-dominant hand, thumb and forefinger down the cord as you are twisting.

Opposite page:
Plants used for braided samples are NZ Flax, Red Hot Poker and Ginger Lily
Photo by Ruth Woods

BRAIDING

Braiding is a simple technique and quite beautiful when using plant fibre.

Recommended fibres

You will need five strands of fibre which will need to be pliable. These could be NZ Flax, Red Hot Poker, Banana fibre or others that you find with similar qualities. If you are not sure - experiment. You could also use five strands of handmade cordage.

Or you can use one leaf that can be cut into five strands leaving the top joined, this is a technique often used in leatherwork.

Braided pieces can be used as handles and easily combinded with other techniques.

How to braid with 5 strands

Tie your five strands of fibre together or attach to a support.

1. Divide your strands - two on the left side and three on the right. **Image 1**
   Take the outer strand on the right and weave over and under the next two strands on the left. **Image 2**

2. Take the outer strand on the left and weave over and under the next strands on the right. **Image 3**

3. Repeat going under and over from the left to the right. **Image 4**

4. And again from the right to the left. **Image 5**

5. You will now see the braid forming. **Image 6**

Image 1

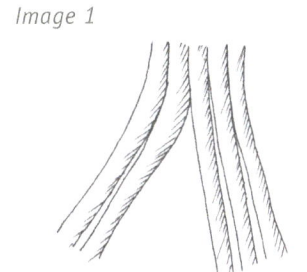

Image 2

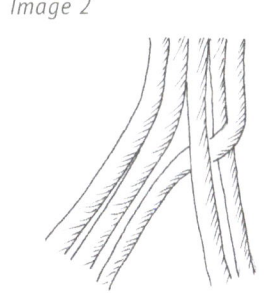

Image 3

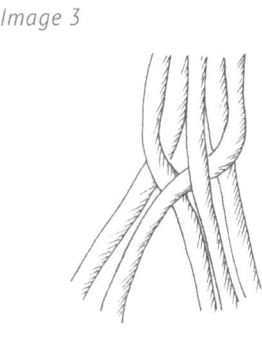

Image 4

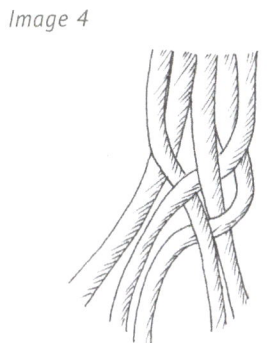

Image 5

Image 6

Opposite page:
A collection of coiled mats using textile waste by Ruth Woods
Photo by Ben Willis

COILING

Coiling is a method that is used worldwide and many different fibres can be incorporated depending on what is accessible.

Coiling starts off at a central point and works in a circle stitching over a core. There are several techniques that can be used. In this section we will use the spiral or overstitch which are similar in method but give quite different results. Other techniques that can be used are 'wrapping stitch', 'blanket stitch' and even crochet which can be worked around a core.

There are many fibres that can be incorporated; flexible materials work best which can include fabric, raffia, soft recycled plastics and of course plant fibres.

Using a combination of plant fibres can add interesting textures and colours.

The work can be shaped according to what is required, can be left flat and used as a mat for functional use, a wall hanging as a decorative piece or moulded to create vessels or sculpture.

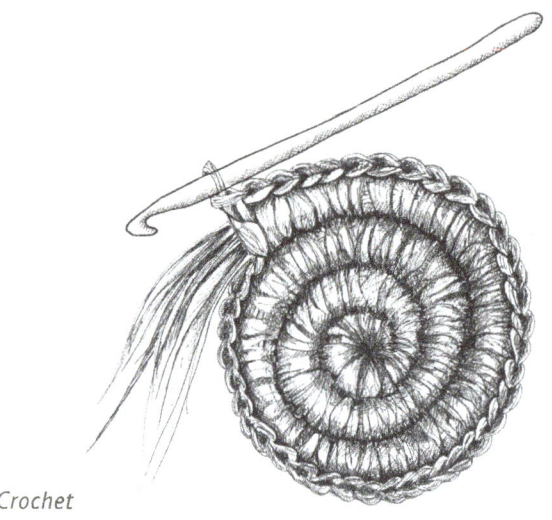
Crochet

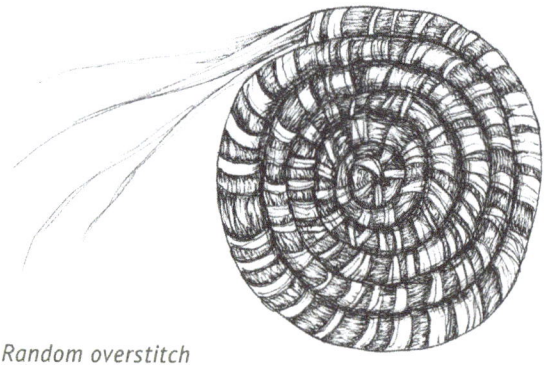
Random overstitch

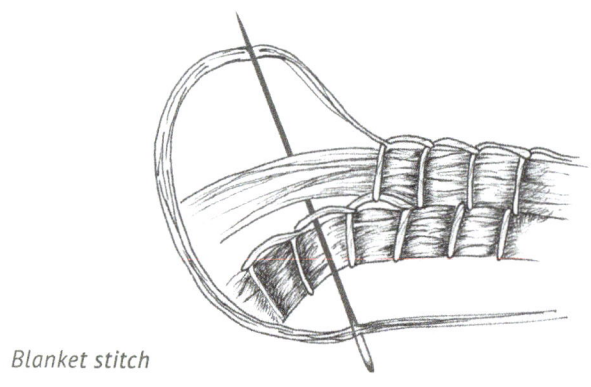
Blanket stitch

Before you start

If your work doesn't look neat or as you would like - do not be concerned. Continue... the more work you create the more confident in your work you will become. A random look has an attractive appeal in basketry - also some basketry techniques are very forgiving and you will find that a basketry piece with a few mistakes will look great.

You will need

- Fibre of your choice - plant fibre, fabric, raffia or recycled soft plastic.

- Strong thread which can be string, cotton yarn, linen thread or waxed linen thread. You can also use NZ flax split finely to 1 - 2 mm as it is very strong and works well as a stitching thread. If your stitching thread is thin you might need to double it.

- A largish needle with a large eye that can take the thread - a darning or large chenille needle.

This technique can be used in a number of ways and can look quite different depending on the materials used and where you place your stitches. You can create a very neat spiral pattern by positioning the stitches in a regular planned way. Alternatively you can stitch in a more random fashion, which is great for beginners and creates a more intuitive piece with very different and appealing outcomes. The latter gives you great scope to experiment with using different materials and threads. If you try both ways you'll be surprised at what can be achieved.

Sometimes it's good to start in a more random way which enables you to learn as you go along. You might see the spiral pattern emerging and you can choose whether to keep it or not.

CREATIVITY IS INVENTING, EXPERIMENTING, GROWING, TAKING RISKS, BREAKING RULES, MAKING MISTAKES AND HAVING FUN

Mary Lou Cook

Emerge by Kate Dick
Photo by Kate Dick
Fibres: Raffia

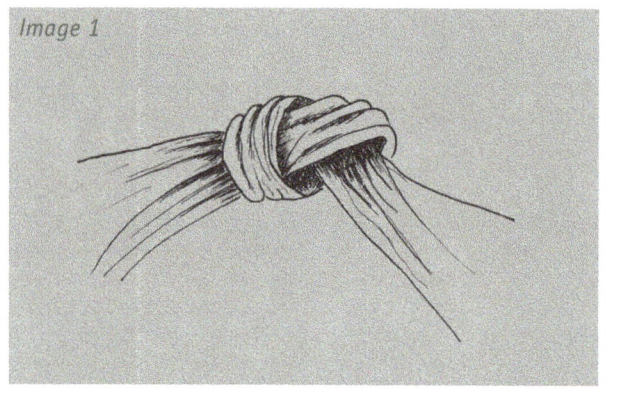

Image 1

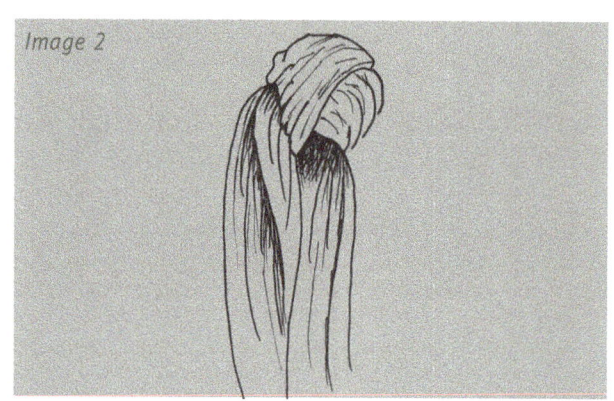

Image 2

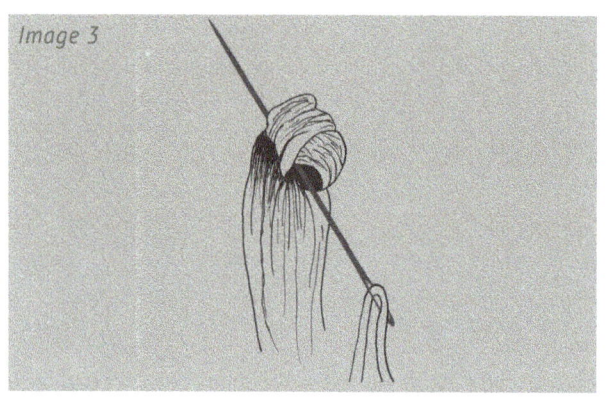

Image 3

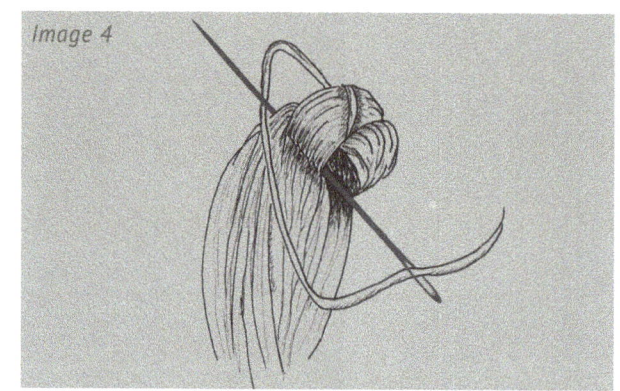

Image 4

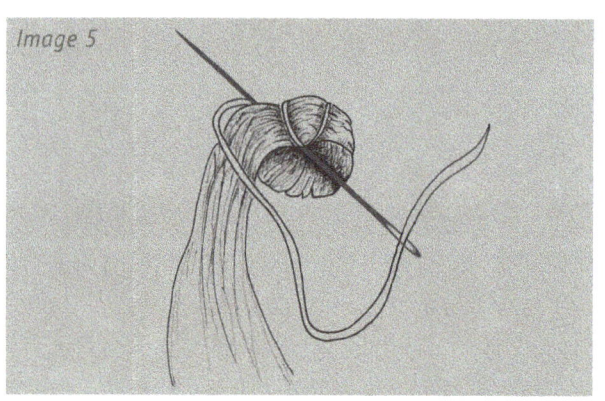

Image 5

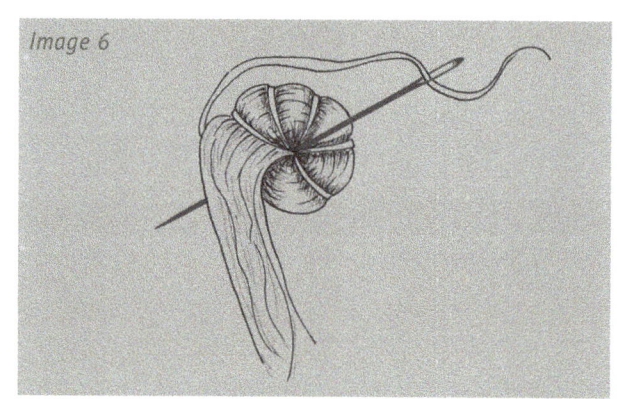

Image 6

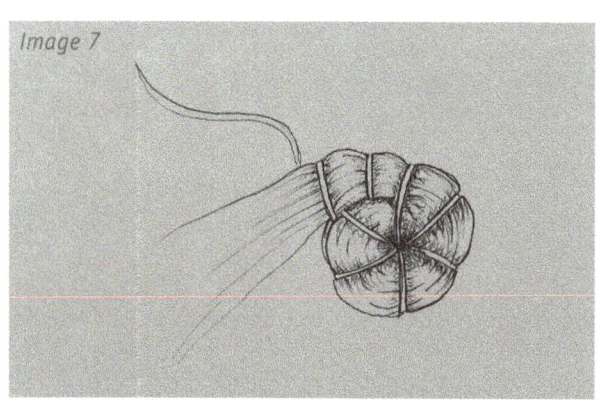

Image 7

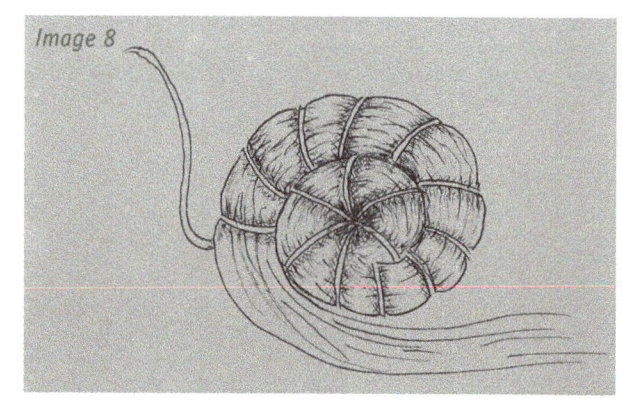

Image 8

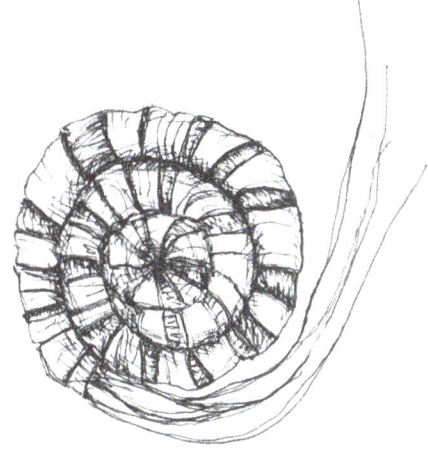

Overstitch and spiral stitch - how to start, grow, shape and finish

1. There are many ways to start, this is just one of them using a simple knot, pull firmly but not too tight. **Image 1**
   After tying the knot, pull the two lengths of fibre down, this will be known as the core, and position the knot at the top. **Image 2**
   Push your threaded needle through the centre of the hole in the knot from the front. Pull the thread through until 10 cm remain - place this thread in the core to be hidden. **Image 3**

2. Next we will start to stitch with an overstitch or spiral stitch. If you are right-handed stitch in an anti-clockwise direction. Hold your work with the two lengths, the core, of fibre in your left hand and stitch with your right.

   Bring the thread over the work and push the needle through the centre of the knot working front to back. **Image 4**
   Create approximately six stitches in this circle working in an anti-clockwise direction - space them out evenly using your thumb to position the stitches. This can be a bit fiddly, however as you make more starter circles you will become better at creating them. **Image 5&6**

   What you want to achieve is to double the number of stitches in this circle. You will do this by placing a stitch above the stitch in the previous round as well as one in between. **Image 7**
   When stitching, place the needle one third into the previous round. Space stitches evenly if you want and occasionally check the back of the work to ensure you've caught all the fibres. **Image 8**

3. When you continue to coil and add stitches where needed - this will be when the gap increases and you can see the space is becoming too wide. If you do this you will create a spiral pattern thus calling it a spiral stitch. If you prefer you can be more strategic and insert more stitches on round four or five.

4. If you create your stitches more randomly you won't have a spiral but you will have a strong overstitch which looks very appealing and creates a great coiled piece. The random stitch is a great technique to experiment with colour and fibre. **See page 137**

5. Continue coiling until you create the required size.

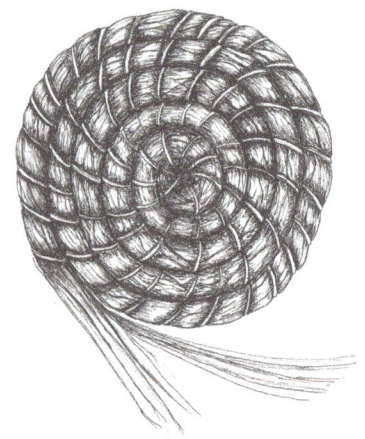

Adding an extra thread for stitching

When your stitching thread has nearly ran out, unthread your needle and place that thread into the core of your work. Take a new thread and start to stitch, leaving the last 10 cm of the new thread in the core of the work.

Adding more core fibre

Add more fibre as required by overlapping the thinning end with the new fibre. Experiment by adding various plant fibres which could give you different textures in your finished work and making it unique.

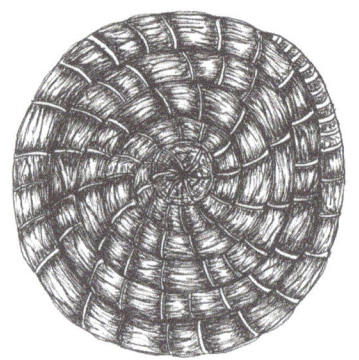

Finishing off

When you are ready to finish off your work leave about 5 - 7 cm before you actually want to finish. Start to taper your work by trimming the core and allow to gradually peter out. As the core diminishes, stitch closer together until the stitching is flush with the previous round. To finish off, pull the thread through the core of your work on the previous round in the same direction as you are stitching.

The overstitch can be used in varying ways and these three examples show the different results obtained when using the one stitch.

In the blue piece you can clearly see by placing the thread in a specific position you can create a beautiful spiral. The green piece used raffia as a thread and by placing the stitches much closer together, it has a more compacted look. The vessel at the top is an example of a more random approach, it uses a random overstitch.

All three pieces were made by Catriona McLean. Photos by Catriona McLean.

Opposite page:
Sculptural Bowl by Anna Whitelaw
Photo by Anna Whitelaw
Fibres: Red Anther Wallaby Grass, Rytidosperma pallium, Poa labillardieri and sheep fleece, stitched with Lomandra and raffia

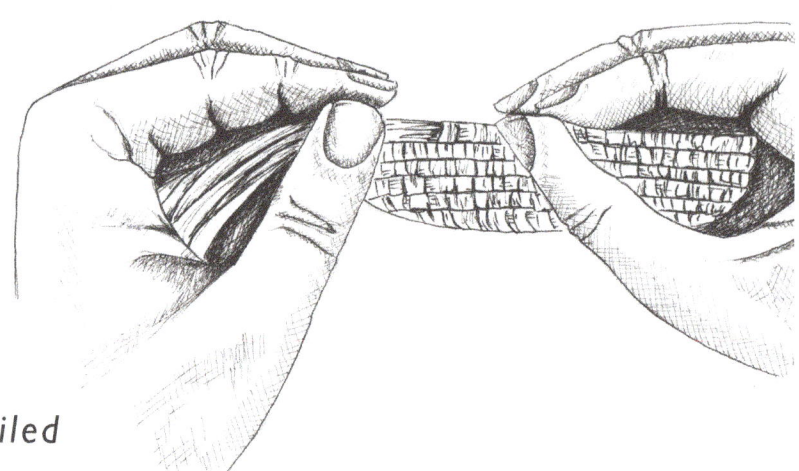

Shaping the curve in a coiled piece

There are a few ways to shape your work. One is to mould the work with your hands, pushing the rounds you are working on away from you as the outside of the work is the side facing you. If you are shaping to a much smaller size, you will need to reduce your stitches but if you are making the work larger you will need to increase your stitches.

Using a mould is another way of assisting to shape your work. Find a bowl to the size you want, lay the work over the bowl and push it into shape. Continue to do this every few rounds and you'll end up with a nicely curved shaped piece.

Keeping your work flat

If you require a piece to stay flat and it starts to curve before you want it to, place it on a table and push it down with your hands. Keep doing this for every round. If your work is a bit larger and it starts to curl, place the work under a few heavy books overnight.

There is nothing like experience and the more you make the more you will learn. Your first few pieces might not be exactly what you want - freeform work can make great sculptures.

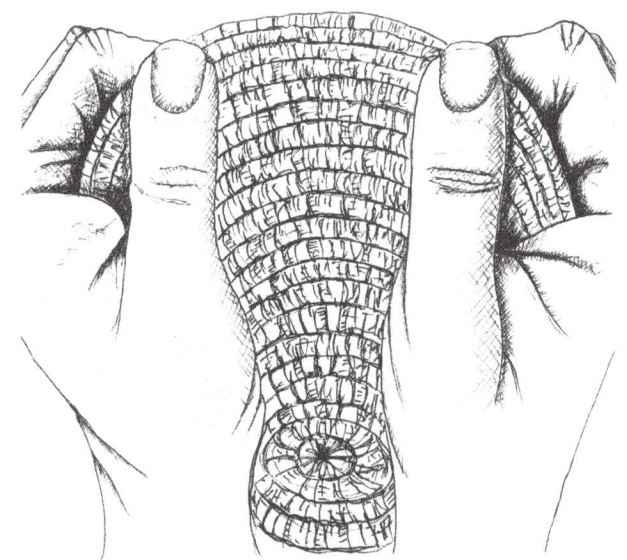

This page:
A beautifully shaped coiled piece using raffia by Kate Dick
Photo by Kate Dick
Fibres: Raffia

This page:
Weaving samples by Helle Jorgensen
Photo by Helle Jorgensen

WEAVING

Weaving can be a generic term used for basketmaking and cloth. There are many techniques for weaving basketry and it can take on many forms. In this section we will look at the basic under-and-over technique which is one of the simplest methods and one you've probably made at school with paper or plastic raffia yarn.

We will also examine twining, a method where two threads are used at the same time.

Elements of the techniques

Both methods use spokes and weavers. The spokes need to be stronger than the weavers and the weavers need to be flexible enough to weave around the spokes. If plant fibre is going to be used for the weavers, you will need to dampen the fibres first so they don't crack or break.

Fibres that can be used

Many materials can be used depending on the outcome required.

For spokes, generally firm strong fibres are preferable whether they be plant-based or recycled materials. Some softer plant fibres and handmade cordage can be used for both spokes and weavers but will have a softer structure.

Plants for spokes can include sticks, vines and stronger leathery leaves such as NZ Flax, *Cordyline australis* and *Agave attenuata*. Palm inflorescence and Jacaranda leaf stalks are suitable and more woody.

For the weavers, you will need flexible materials which could include the softer leaf plants and other fibres such as soft plastics or recycled fabric. Plants could include Daylilies, Daffodils, Watsonia, Chasmanthe, Red Hot Poker and generally plants with a softer structure.

Check out the Materials section of this book for inspiration.

Under-and-over weaving

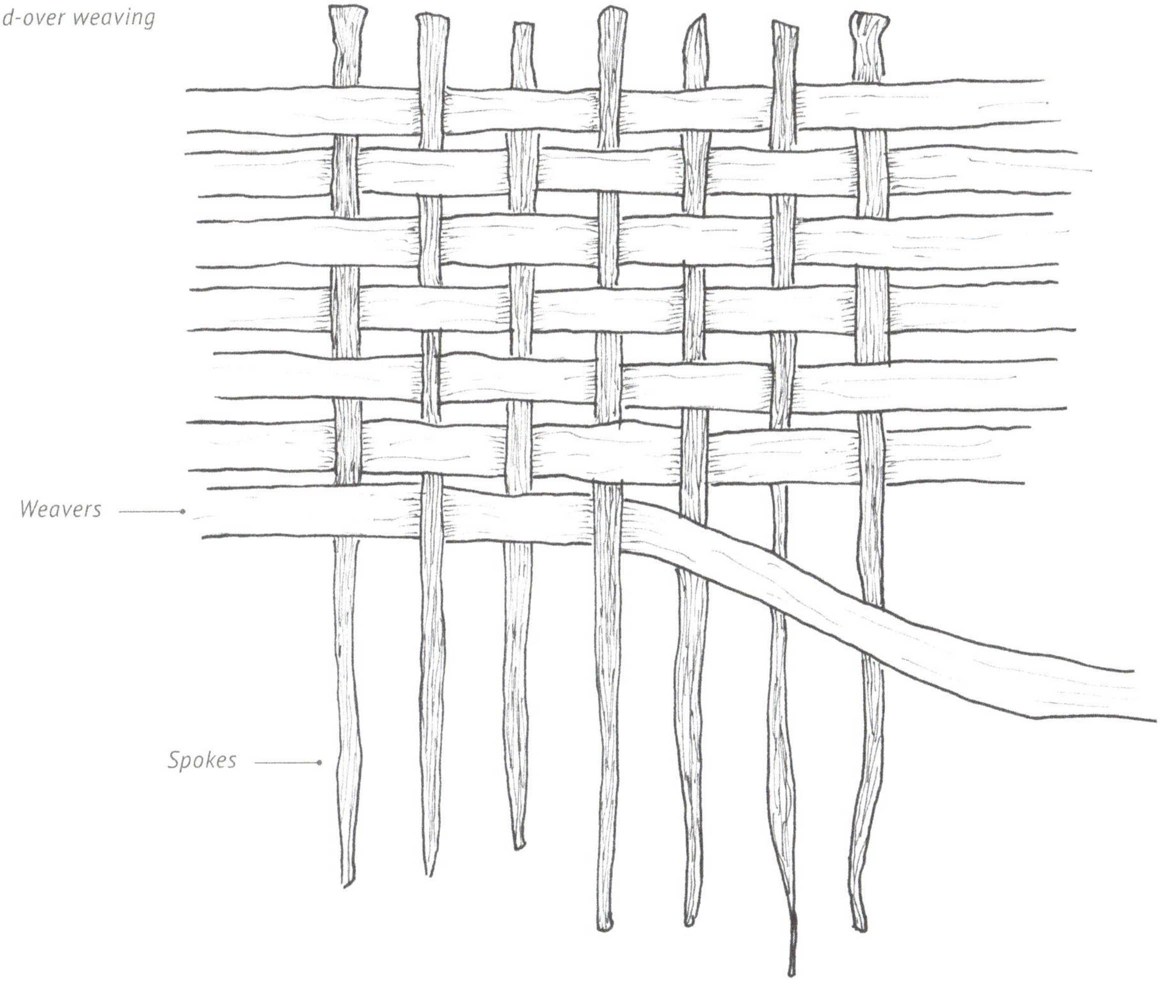

Weavers

Spokes

Twining

Weavers

Spokes

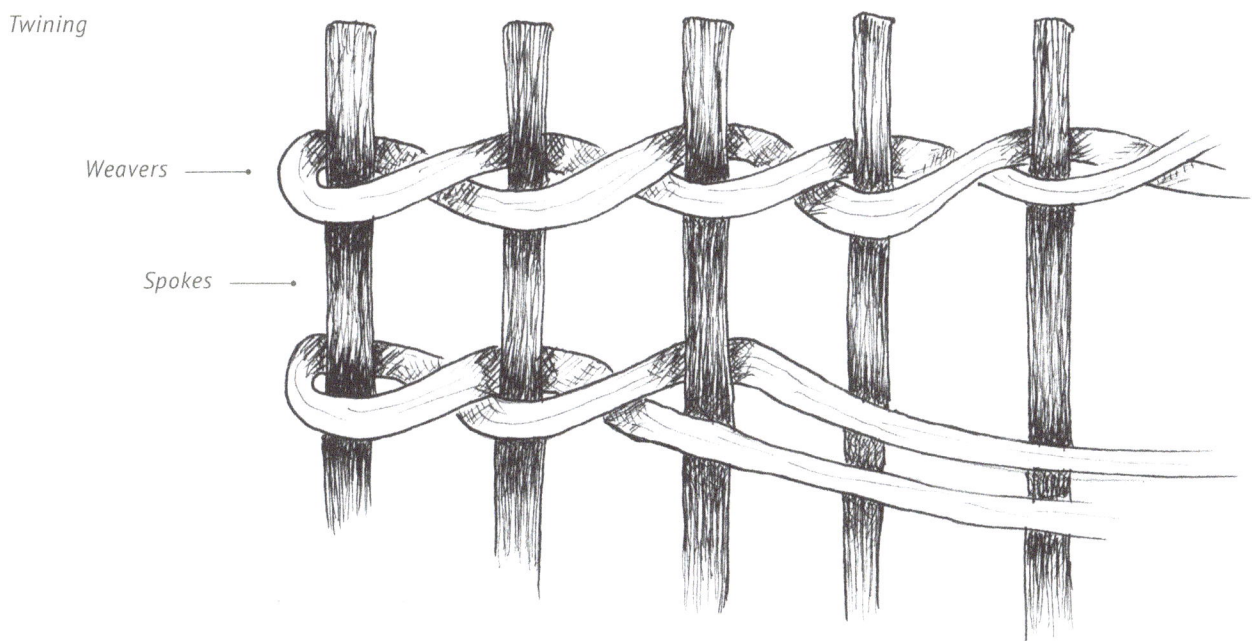

141

This page, clockwise from top left:
Under-and-over technique 1
Photo by Ruth Woods
Fibres: Eucalyptus bark and Pittosporum tenuifolium

Under-and-over technique 2
Photo by Ruth Woods
Fibres: Cordyline australis and Red Hot Poker

Opposite page:
Simple woven forms
Photo by Sean Paris
Fibres: NZ flax, Red Hot Poker and Billy Button flowers

Examples of under and over weaving

These two pieces were created as samples to explore the under and over method using quite different plant materials.

The piece above has been made using bark and fine twigs. The twigs have been used as individual lengths and woven with the ends sticking out creating a very rustic appearance.

The piece to the right has used Red Hot Poker as the weaver, which is a soft long strappy leaf plant and a *Cordyline Australis* for the spokes. The weaver has been continually woven backwards and forwards until the leaf has run out. This gives a much smoother appearance. See following pages.

Image 1 - Starting

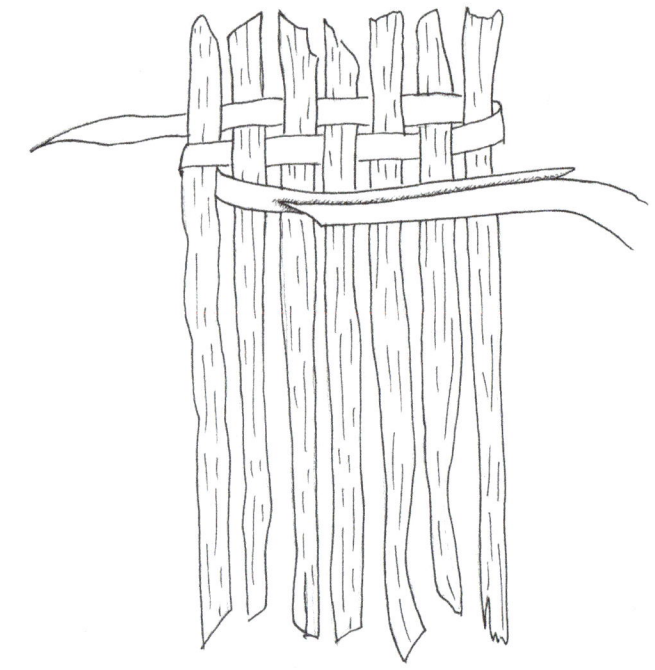

Image 2 - Adding

Image 3 - Back

Image 4 - Front

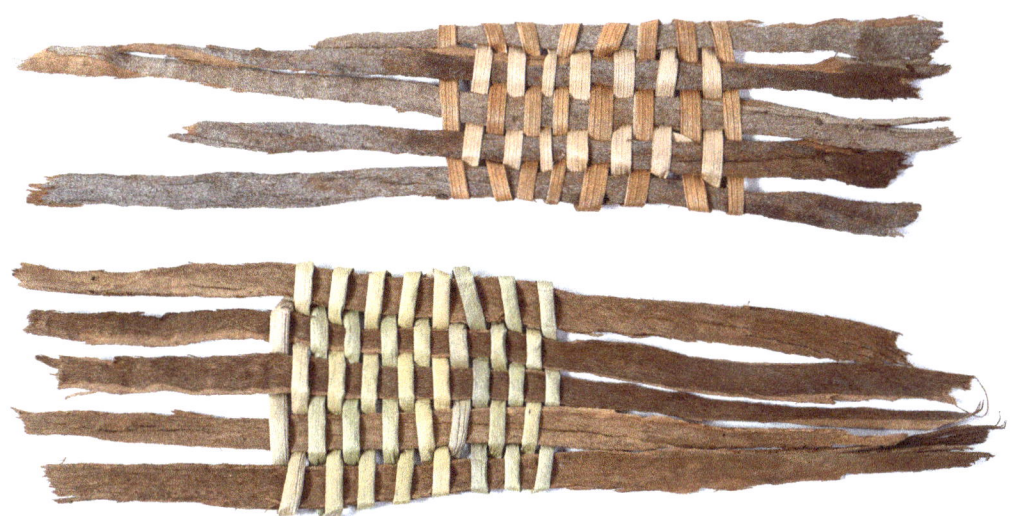

Under-and-over

This is one of the easiest techniques and can be constructed and used in many forms.

1. Using spokes and weavers we will select an odd number of spokes.

2. Lay your spokes on the table. You might need to tape them down to start with to keep them in place - the tape can be removed later.

3. Use one of your soft weavers and simply go under and over each spoke as in the diagram. **Image 1**

4. You can finish at the end of the row and leave the end of the weaver sticking out as a feature - then use a new weaver starting with the opposite spoke.

5. Alternatively, continue weaving using the same weaver and when you reach the end of the row, turn around and come back the opposite way, weaving under and over opposite spokes. **Image 2**

6. Push up the weavers as you go along to fill in the gaps.

7. Keep going until your weaver has run out. **Image 2**

8. If you want to continue, you can introduce a new weaver.

9. Blend the new weaver with the old weaver when weaving the last few spokes and weave as one until the old weaver has run out. Continue weaving with the new weaver.

10. To finish off, thread the weaver end up through the other rows on the reverse side of the work. **Image 3**

Image 1

Image 2

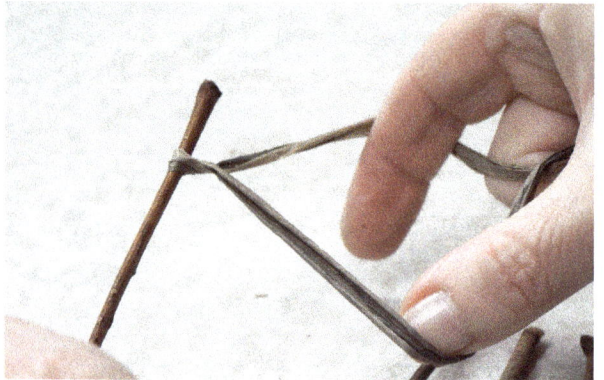
Image 3

Image 4

Image 5

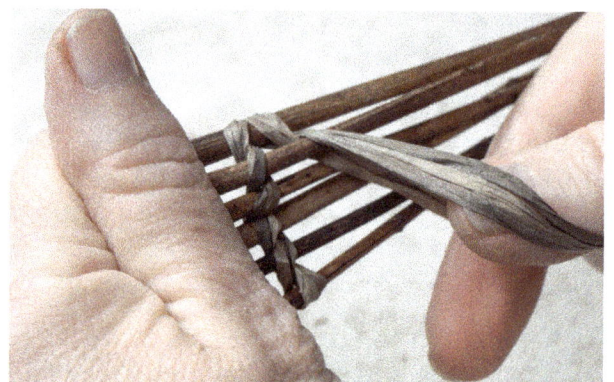
Image 6

Image 7

Image 8

Twining

1. Select the sticks (spokes) you want to use - here we have used Jacaranda leaf stalks. **Image 1**

2. Select the fibre (weavers) you would like to use - something soft and pliable and might need to be dampened or soaked before using. Bulrush, a tall sedge, Banana fibre, string or even raffia can be used.

3. Divide your weaver in half but slightly off-centre by a few centimetres.

4. Loop around the first stick. **Image 2**

5. Twist the weaver towards you once. **Image 3**

6. Then insert a spoke next to first spoke with the twist in between. Hold firmly and pull the weavers tightly as you repeat twisting the threads towards you, adding spokes as you go. **Image 4**

7. Repeat this until you have as many spokes as you require. If you have not done this before use maybe 5 or 7 spokes to practice with.

8. If you run out of the weaver thread simply place a new one on top of the weaver that is running out and weave as one piece for about four spokes - enough to keep it secure. As the old weaver runs out the new one will take its place.

9. When you get to the end, twist and work back the opposite way. **Images 5 & 6**

10. To finish, pull the weaver back down through the previous row. **Image 8**

You could incorporate many different types of fibres creating an interesting practice piece.

LOOPING

Looping can create varied looking work - the method we are creating is a simple half hitch knot looped into itself.

The history of looping can be seen from many First Nations people from around the world including PNG, Australia, Europe and South America.

There are several techniques to create simple bags and nets used for fishing and other food gathering tasks.

What you can use

Handmade cordage or commercial string, strips of fabric and even soft plastics can be used to create a looped piece.

Most soft plant and soft recycled fibres outlined in this book are able to produce cordage.

What follows is just one simple method of looping. It is versatile and ideal for flat work or working on a round piece.

Before you start

If this is the first time you've created a looped piece, make it small - no bigger than 15 cm wide for a flat piece and 10 cm in diameter. Practise the technique before embarking on larger works to become familiar with the technique.

When using commercial string you will need to cut into approximately 1.5 metre lengths and join when you run out with a sheet bend knot, see below.

Sheet bend knot to tie two fibres securely together.

Using handmade cordage

If you are using handmade cordage as you are looping, make about 2 meters of cord to start with, work your loops as required, when you have run out of cord, make another metre or so. This way you will have a piece of work with no joining knots - just a continuous piece of cordage.

 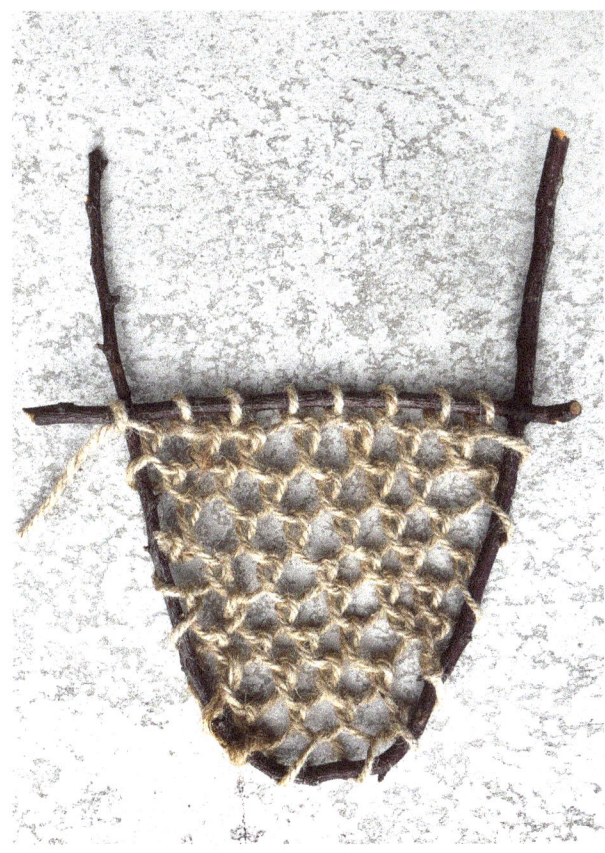

You will need

- Commercial string / thread such as linen or cotton thread 1 mm plus or similar. You might need to experiment to see what works best.

- Something to make a frame such as a couple of bendable branches. Approximately 1 x 20 cm and 1 x 50 cm

- You might find a needle with a big eye, a darning needle or something similar is an advantage if your thread is soft.

- Fibre for handmade cord if you choose this method - see Making the cord section on page 127.

Frame

You will need a flat frame to work on. Create a flat frame with two small branches. One short one at the top and a longer bendable one. Join the sticks together by bending the long one around like the image and tie to hold in place.

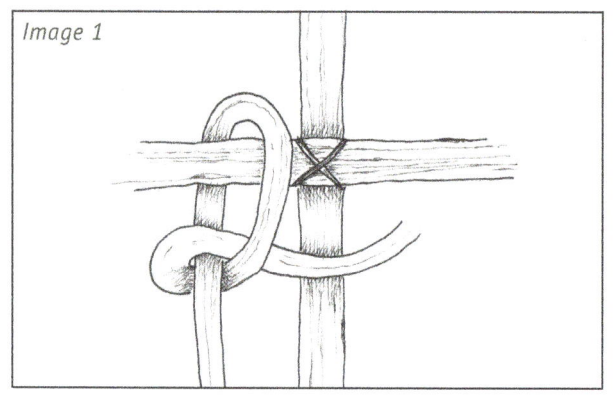

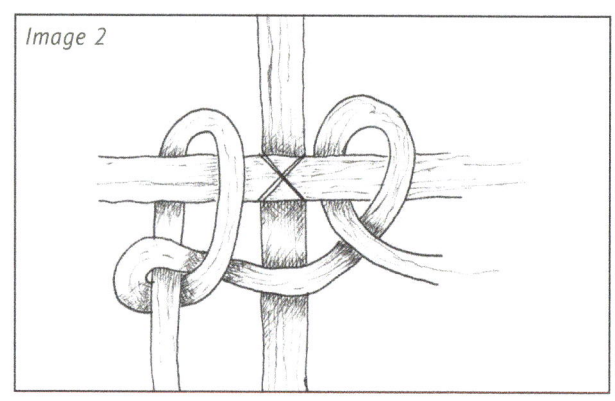

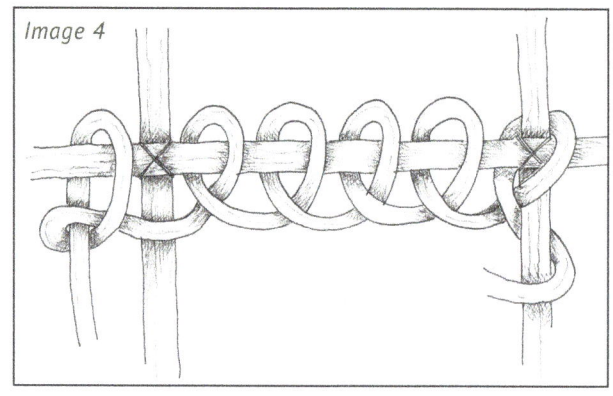

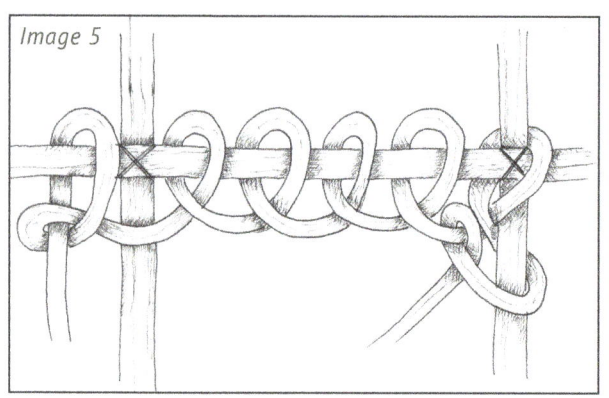

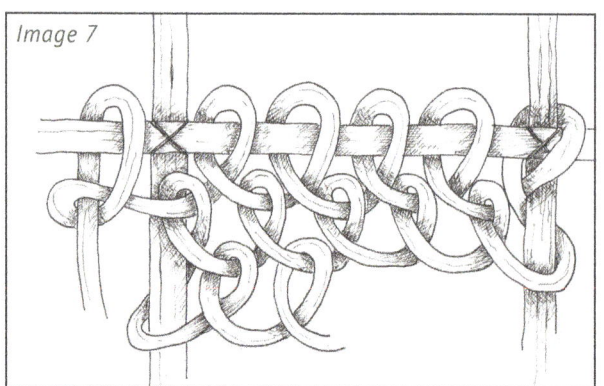

Opposite page:
Vine structure and looping with waxed linen thread.
Photo by Ben Willis

How to loop with a frame

1. Tie a simple knot as shown to the left side of the attached stick. **Image 1**

2. Make your first loop on the right side of the attached stick going over from the front to the back, then coming down through the loop created. This is called a Half Hitch Knot. **Image 2**

3. Continue these loops across the stick spacing them out evenly, don't bunch them up too close or make them too tight or you won't be able to loop the next row. **Image 3**

4. When you get to the end, loop around where the sticks join. **Image 4**

5. Start to loop in the other direction BUT this time you will go through the loops from behind to the front then thread through the newly formed loop. **Image 5**

6. Continue looping this way until you get to the end. **Image 6**

7. Turn, looping around the frame, you will now loop from the front to the back.

8. If you run out of thread and want to continue use a sheet bend knot to join. Try and keep your knots at the end.

9. When you want to finish, stop at one end and tie off on the stick with two loops and pull your string up through the loops on the stick.

RANDOM WEAVE

Random weave is an excellent technique to start a basketry journey.

A piece can be created quite quickly in a few hours and improves when the creator understands what makes a firm piece and how to manipulate the form. It is a very satisfying process and can easily be turned into interesting sculptures.

Calling it random weave is not really an accurate description as there is a rhythm to the process which keeps it stable, firm and flexible. Random weave is an excellent technique to use for sculpture as you can manipulate the shape quite easily. There are many ways to create a random weave piece and each person who uses this technique will use a different method.

Robyn Norris is a Melbourne atist whose work is inspired by the Australian bush and combining that beauty into her craft.

This page:
Sprouts by Robyn Norris
Photo by Ben Willis
Fibres: Rusted wire

Opposite page:
Princess Glory by Robyn Norris
Photo by Ben Willis
Fibre: Silver Princess (Eucalytpus caesia)

This page:
Sleeping it Off by Fleur Brett
Photo by Theresa Harrison
Fibre used: Reclaimed data cable

Opposite page:
Example of random weave ball by Ruth Woods
Photo by Ben Willis
Fibre: Lomandra - Mat-Rush

I was taught two techniques of Random weave. Lesley Hall showed me the thicker weave using vines or branches and Marion Gaemers taught me the finer method using fine fibres like Mat-Rush.

Fibres that can be used

A huge variety of materials can be used from very fine grasses to much thicker fibres like vines and flexible branches. The finished piece depends greatly on the materials used.

For soft, fine, random woven pieces, NZ Flax (*Phormium tenax*), Lomandra or Mat-Rush, or similar plants can be used by splitting the leaves into fine ribbons 1 - 2 mm wide. These can be used immediately or bundled into round coils, dried and used later.

Woody type plants can be picked green but must be dried first before use as the shrinkage will be great and the work will become unstable. Bundle into coils and once dried, you can use when ready by soaking until pliable.

Electrical cable and soft fabrics, paper cord can also be used and obviously will give a totally different result.

Random weave with fine fibre

The objective of creating this technique is to make a lattice type structure with many strands of fibre woven in and out of the work. Some strands will be woven in a circular direction throughout the work and others in a straight direction. This will create a strength within the structure which is what you need.

At the beginning it may feel like the work is messy, not growing and doesn't feel stable. The key is to keep going and weave under and over as many fibres as possible - this will create a good firm base to work with.

Plant materials you can use

You will need Lomandra, NZ Flax or similar long leaved plants. Start off with 20 leaves and split length ways 1 - 2 mm wide with a needle or your fingernail. With this technique you don't have to let the fibres dry.

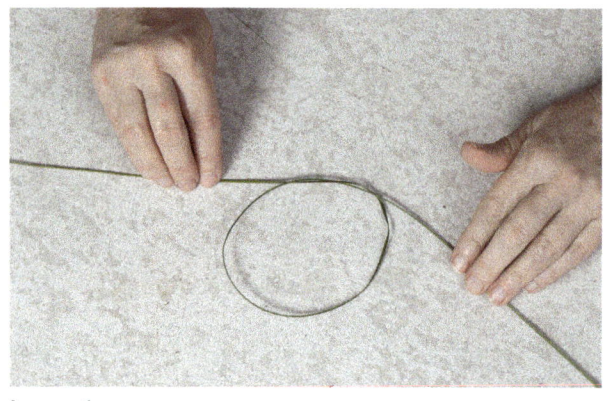
Image 1

Image 2

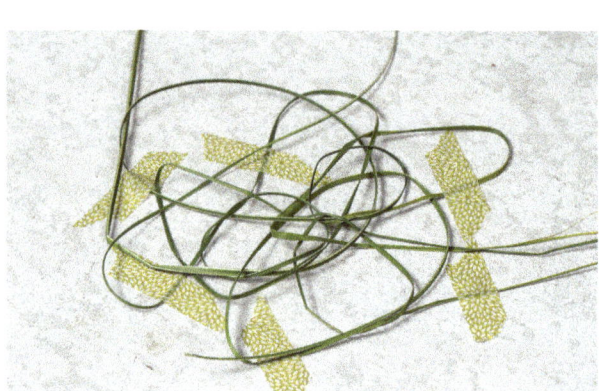
Image 3

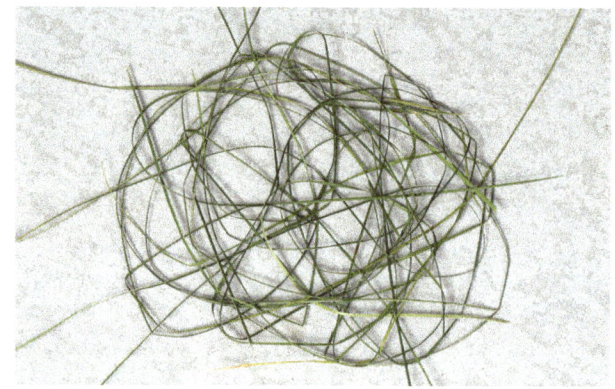
Image 4

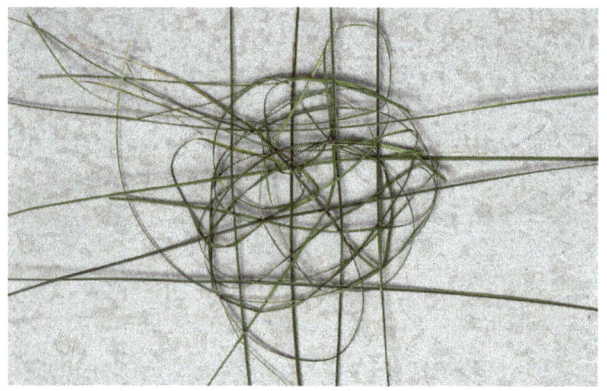
Image 5

Image 6

Image 7

Image 8

Image 9

Image 10

Image 11

Image 12

How to random weave with fine fibres

Think about the shape you want - a ball or a bowl shape is probably the easiest to start with.

1. Make a single loop with one strand of fibre. **Image 1**

2. Make two more loops and join together so the circles are linked in a triangle. To make it easier you can tape the beginning of the work onto a board. **Image 2**

3. With the strand ends weave back into the circles making sure you go under and over the threads as much as possible. **Image 3**

4. Then add more strands of the existing piece, weaving under and over as much as possible as before, bringing the long ends back into the work - don't pull them tight - you can probably take the tape off now as the work should be firm enough to hold itself. **Image 4**

5. Add new strands both horizontally and vertically going under and over as before. Doing this will add to the strength of the base creating a lattice type structure. **Image 5**

6. Keep weaving the existing strands evenly throughout the work - stand back and look from a distance to see if it looks even - continue to fill in where the gaps are.

7. Then add strands going around the work weaving under and over. **Image 6**

8. Make loops with the strands to the side to make the piece bigger - filling in the gaps as you go.

9. Keep adding and doing the same technique until you have the size you want to work with.

10. When you have a reasonably filled in mat base - you can start to shape your work. **Image 7**

11. Take your mould (this can be a ball or a bowl), hold it firm and start to manipulate the strands by pushing and pulling with your hands around the mould. You will feel the fibres moving. **Image 8**

12. Keep adding more strands while the work is around the mould, pushing it into shape. **Image 9**

13. Remember to leave the top open so you can remove the mould. **Image 10**

14. Once you are happy with the shape, take the mould out and continue to manipulate to the shape required. **Image 11**

15. If you want a ball shape, pull the threads over the top and try and replicate the sphere for the top. **Image 12**

16. You might like to pull all the threads to the top like a ponytail and wrap the tail with more fibre as shown. **Image 13**

17. To finish off, weave in the loose threads and tidy the top loose threads by weaving them in, or leave them loose as a feature.

You can replicate this process using other shapes or making it more freeform. You can also join shapes together, attaching them by weaving under and over with more strands. Keep adding strands until the pieces are securely fixed together. Try experimenting with other shape moulds.

Image 13

This page and pages 156 - 157:
Fine random weave instructions
Photos by Ben Willis

Random weave using thicker fibre

Plant materials you can use

There are numerous plant fibres that can be used for random weave including branches from Willow, fruit tree pruning, Wisteria, Dogwood, Eucalyptus and many vines.

Preparation

It is recommended that branches are used freshly cut before they start to dry out. This way they are flexible and easier to manipulate. When weaving you will need to pack the branches tightly so when they dry out the structure doesn't become loose. If they do, you can add extra branches to firm the piece up again.

Using vines, you will need to pick and bundle them into round coils and leave to dry for at least a few months. When ready to use soak overnight which enables them to be flexible again.

Image 1

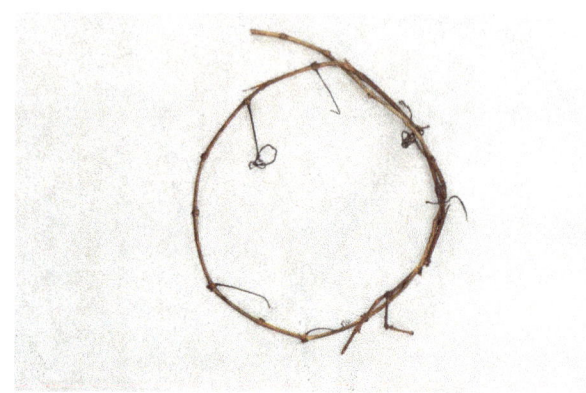
Image 2

Image 3

Image 4

Image 5

Image 6

Image 7

Image 8

How to make a random weave ball with grapevine

If you cannot access the same plant fibre I have used - try something similar and experiment. If you don't have the same lengths, use shorter and make a smaller piece. The measurements are meant as a guide.

1. Collect about twenty five - thirty lengths measuring 1.5 metres (50") of grapevine or similar. I have soaked them overnight to make them pliable. **Image 1**

2. Make three hoops about 30 cm (12") in diameter. **Image 2**

3. Insert one hoop inside the other crossing over at the top and bottom. Tie at these crossing points. You can use cable ties which are very tough and can be cut off later or you can use strong thread. **Image 3**

4. Place a third loop horizontally and tie securely at crossing points again. This now gives you a frame to work with. **Image 4**

5. Using your soaked vine stems, start to weave under and over the frame as much as possible. **Image 5**

6. While doing so, continue to look at where the stems are being placed - keep it evenly balanced with the same amount of weaving around the piece.

7. Stop and look at your work at regular intervals to check where the gaps need filling with the vines. If the shape looks one-sided or out of place, squash it into shape by gently pushing down on top or using two hands on either side of the work squashing together. This is important to do as you are making the ball because the more dense the piece becomes the harder to reshape. **Images 6 & 7**

8. Keep weaving under and over throughout the piece making a firm structure. **Images 8 - 10**

Once you are happy with your piece you can call it finished. You might like to leave it on show so you can look at it for a while and add to it if you feel it needs some extra pieces added.

If you have made this with freshly picked branches and after a while it becomes loose - you can add more to make it firmer. The more vines or branches you include the firmer it will be.

This page, opposite page and 159:
Random weave with grapevine instructions

Photos by Sean Paris

Image 9

Image 10

A God's eye made from handmade plant cordage. It's another way to connect two branches together securely.

This page and opposite page:
Photos by Sean Paris

CREATING FORM

CREATING A STRUCTURE

In this section we will make two basic structures which will allow you to add any of the methods from the Techniques section.

These structures can be made with other materials such as wire, plastic or fabric as long as you have a sturdy framework in place.

You can create different structures by changing the construction, making them taller, shorter or any unique shape.

As we have discussed throughout the book it's all about playing and experimenting to see what works.

Creating a frame with hoops and loops

Creating a framework with branches or vines takes a little preparation but is well worth it.

Collect your branches ahead of time. I usually collect mine when I see someone pruning or removing a tree. Freshly cut branches work best as they are flexible and easy to use.

If you are using vines you will probably be able to find longer lengths. I use Ivy and grapevine but most vines should be suitable. You can cut and bundle them in a coil and store for later use.

Although you might feel impatient and want to get started straight away the preparation is certainly an advantage. Nevertheless if you just want to try it out and can't wait to create your framework you can always re-tie the connecting points later as they will become loose as they shink (I have done this).

What you will need

The length of your branches will determine the size of the piece.

For the loops (uprights) 3 - 4 freshly cut branches 1 metre (40") approximately, about the thickness of your middle finger at the thick end of the branch. I have allowed a couple of extras in case some snap.

For the hoops 3 - 4 finer branches, 80 cm and the width of a pen.

Waxed thread, this works best to secure the connection of the branches. If you don't have any, you can make your own with thread, cotton crochet thread or a linen thread, cut thread into one metre lengths and pull through a block of beeswax. Or you can use strong thread but make sure to tie the connections firmly.

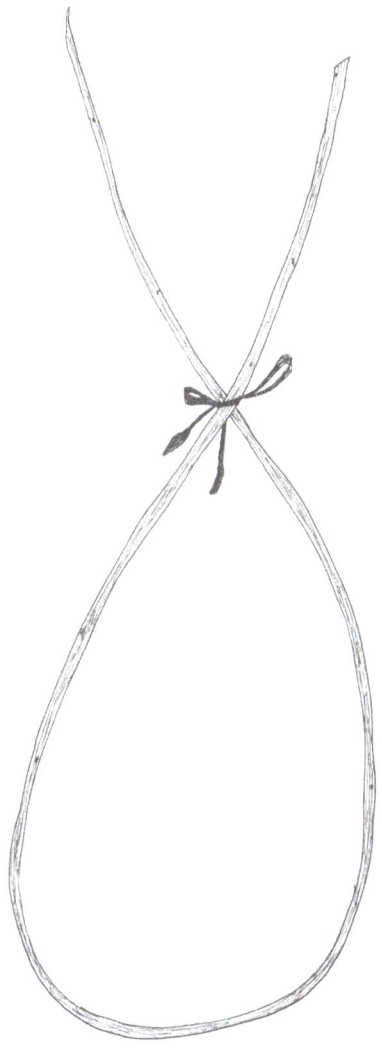

Image 1

Image 2

Making the framework

1. While the branches are still fresh, bend into a loop and tie firmly with ordinary string about one third of the way down. **Image 1**

2. This needs to be held in place until the branch has dried, usually about a month, then the loop will hold its shape. If you have enough branches, make a few so you can create several structures at a time.

3. With the finer branches, make three or four hoops for each structure by twisting them into wreath shaped circles. **Image 2**

4. These will need to be a size that fit into the looped branches that have been made. You can assist them to form a nice circle by placing them around a plant pot to dry out. **See photo above**

Make them slightly different sizes - approximately 25 cm, 20 cm and 15 cm (12", 10" and 15"). These do not have to be accurate - they are just a guide of decreasing sizes - they might be smaller if you are making a smaller structure. By making extra you have a few to experiment with. Let them dry out also.

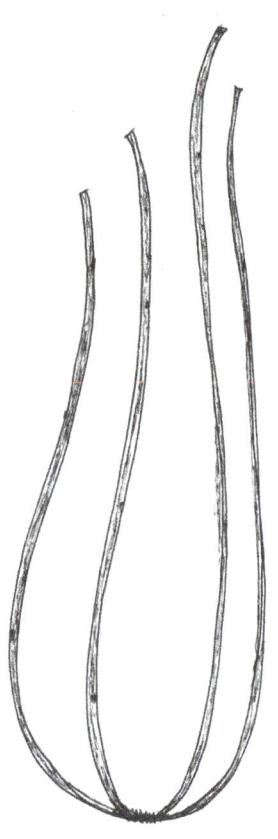

With your prepared hoops and loops you can start to assemble the framework.

5. Take your loops, cross them over and secure them at the base by firmly tying with waxed thread. This will be permanent and not removed. **Image 3**

6. Select your hoops and place them inside the structure and work out where they will be best placed sizewise. Usually the largest hoop will be at the bottom or in the middle of the structure and the smaller sized hoops at the top. **Image 4**

7. Securely tie at all the connecting points with waxed thread making sure they are spaced out evenly and parallel, depending on your design. This now gives you a base structure to work with. **Images 5 & 6**

Image 3

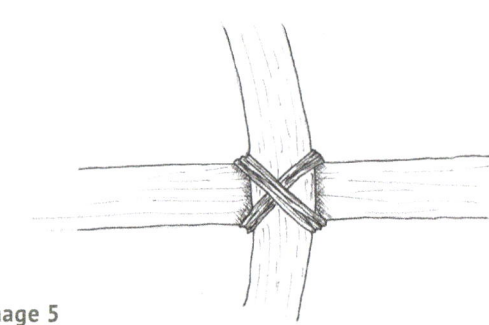

Image 5

Image 4

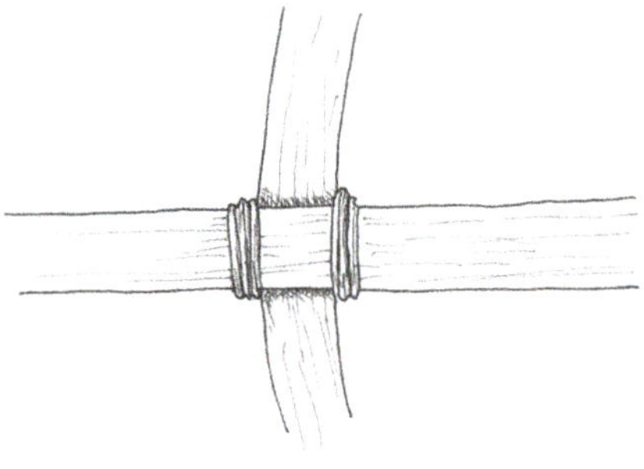

Image 6

Frame made from branches of a plum tree. Section filled in with NZ Flax using the twining technique.
Photo by Sean Paris

You might also like to add extra uprights using interesting shaping sticks, which will divide up the sections more. Tie them in place. Fill in these small sections with the methods you have learnt in the Techniques section of this book.

A collection of freshly picked branches made into hoops and loops, drying, ready to create a sculpture.

Creating a form with hoops and straight branches

For this frame you can use already dried branches but they still need a degree of flexibility.

1. Select nine fine branches about the thickness of a pen; bunch them together at the thick end and tie securely with strong thread. **Image 1**

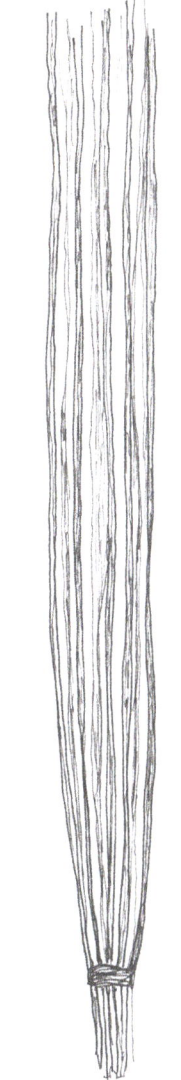

Image 1

Photo by Sean Paris

2. Place two wreath hoops inside the middle of the branches and space them out. Arrange the branches evenly around the hoops. **Image 2**

3. Tie the hoop to each branch in the position you require with strong thread. **Image 3**

4. Tie the other end of the branches together. Now the hoops are enclosed inside the structure. **Image 4**

You can now fill in the sections as you wish with the technique of your choice creating your own design.

Image 3

Image 2

Image 4

Structure created using plum tree branches and filling in the centre section with linen thread.

Photo by Sean Paris

ABOUT THE AUTHOR

CRAFT SCHOOL OZ

BIBLIOGRAPHY

ACKNOWLEDGEMENTS

RESOURCES

FIND ARTISTS AND CONTRIBUTORS

INDEX

ABOUT THE AUTHOR

Ruth has been an adult educator for over 25 years teaching various creative subjects such as accredited art classes, clothing design, art business start-ups and more lately basketry and slow stitching concepts.

Her more recent craft topics came from using materials that were organic or recycled as Ruth is considerably conscious about sustainability and care for the environment.

Much of these materials could be found in Ruth's own cupboards and garden, and also in her own stash of collected craft materials. This philosophy is what drives her own creativity, workshops and teaching.

Ruth is a 'gatherer' and part of her basketry journey began with creating her own garden with a keen eye for plants suitable for weaving and dyeing and has developed what she aptly calls her 'Weaving Pantry' in her home garden. She harvests her plant fibres throughout the seasons of the year.

New Zealand flax is one of her favourites which she can pick fresh from the garden and use immediately to create beautiful organic sculptural forms.

Ruth also has 'secret places' where she collects from good friends that allow her to explore their gardens and choose more unusual plant fibres.

Unlike most gardeners, Ruth looks at plants for their soft and pliable leaves, colour or for length and the flexibility of a twig or branch that enables manipulation into her sculptural forms. She's developed a keen eye through many years of experience travelling along the eastern coast of Australia from cool temperate climates to tropical environments. Plant life varies and excites her interest. She'll pick, dry and give them a try in the exploration of her craft.

Strong influences in Ruth's life began as a child in the UK where her resourceful mother taught her a love of textiles through sewing and knitting. Her older sister, Pamela, gave her an awareness of good fashion style and this led Ruth to study as a clothing designer. She met Kaffe Fassett while studying, and his work has remained an ongoing inspiration.

Other artists that have inspired Ruth are Australian sculptors Bronwyn Oliver, Rosalie Gascoigne and John Davies.

But Mavis Ganambarr, an Indigenous weaver from Elcho Island where Ruth lived and worked, was a humbling turning point. Mavis introduced Ruth to coiling and they spent many weekends as friends coiling with Pandanas fibre together, weaving for hours to make some beautiful pieces.

On returning from Arnhem Land she joined the Basketmakers of Victoria with a hunger to learn more about basketry and the infinite possibilities of plant fibre and techniques. She met many gifted and generous women who shared their knowledge.

This book was developed after going away for a weekend with five other basketry friends, throwing an idea around to showcase a selection of contemporary basketry artists, list of materials and weaving techniques. The project was a little larger than first anticipated and took over three years to produce.

Ruth still continues to explore plant fibre and sculptural form and in 2021 was a finalist for the Yarra Valley Arts & Yering Station Sculpture Award. She continues to explore sculpture with plant fibre and develop more online courses with her son Ben.

This page:
Containment by Ruth Woods
Photo by Ben Willis
Fibres: Mat-Rush, Lomandra

CRAFT SCHOOL OZ

Ruth developed a full time business, Crafts School Oz in 2014 and with her husband Tony traveled up and down the country for three months during winter in their trusty van where Ruth would run workshops along the way. It was a great way to meet people and have craft focused trips but very importantly visit and have time with family.

It would take months to plan these trips, trying to focus on regional areas where often communities wouldn't have opportunities to participate in craft workshops. She was also engaged by larger professional studios to run classes. Ahead of time Ruth would put a call out asking if individuals or groups would like to host a workshop. The itinerary would quickly fill up travelling from Melbourne to Mossman - the very top of Queensland - often travelling over 9000 km around Australia.

In 2019 she was able to combine her face-to-face workshops with online professional videos with the help of her filmmaker son Ben; to share not only locally but worldwide to an audience of keen crafters. Because of Ruth's teaching passion and constant desire to share knowledge she has produced several online workshops. These include various basketry and textile courses. She also has a YouTube channel where people can access free tutorials such as making cord and starter coiled circles. The blog on her website features a variety of makers to highlight dedicated creative makers in the craft community.

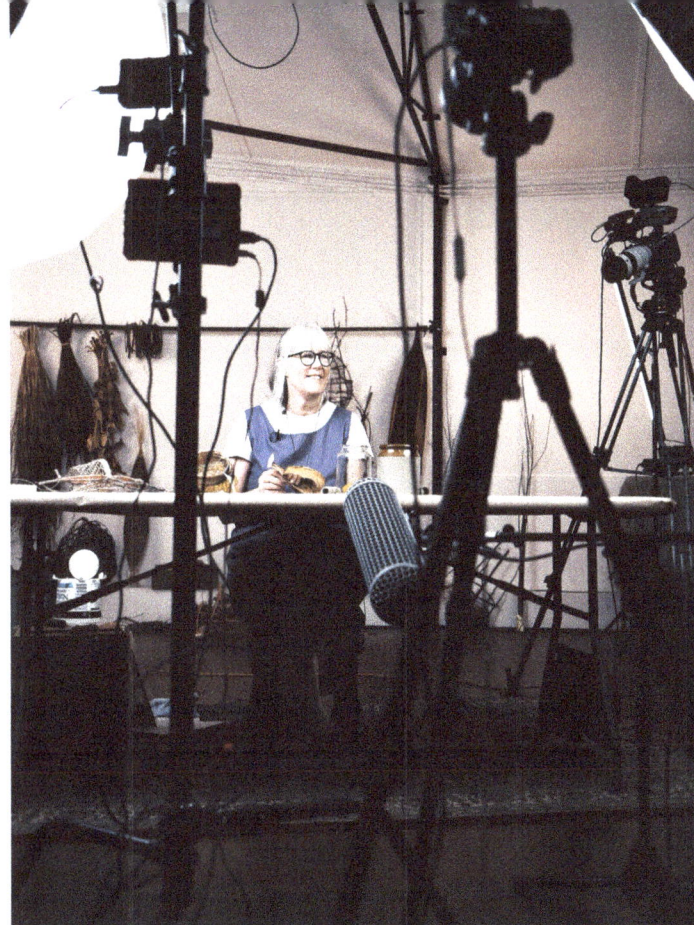

You can enjoy Ruth's courses and YouTube tutorials by exploring the following links:

- www.courses.craftschooloz.com
- www.craftschooloz.com
- www.youtube.com/craftschooloz

You can also contact Ruth by email:
create@craftschooloz.com

BIBLIOGRAPHY

Plants

What to Plant? An illustrated guide for Australian Gardeners	Kristo Pienaar and Denise Greig 1984
Starting out with Palms	David L Jones 2010
Native Grasses for Australian Gardens	Nola Parry and Jocelyn Jones 2007
Native - Art and Design with Australian Plants	Kate Herd & Jela Ivanoviç - Waters 2017

Basketry Books

Fibre Basketry - Homegrown and Handmade	Edited by Helen Richardson 1989
Fibre Basketry Techniques	Averil Otiv 2017
Handmade Baskets - from Nature's colourful materials	Susie Vaughan 1994
Catalogue - Too Weave	Broken Hill City Art Gallery 2000
Woven Forms - Contemporary basketmaking in Australia	Object Gallery NSW 2005
Re Coil Change and Exchange in Coiled Fibre Art	Artback Northern Territory Art Touring 2007
Fabulous Woven Jewellery	Mary Hettmansperger 2006
The Sculpture of Ruth Asawa - contours in the air	Burgard Cornell 2020
The Sculpture of Bronwyn Oliver - Catalogue	Tarrawarra Museum of Art 2016
Bangalow Palm article for Basketry NSW	Glenese Keavney

ACKNOWLEDGEMENTS

I would like to thank and acknowledge the following people. Many people have helped me on this journey over three years to enable this book to become a reality. A weekend away with basketry friends made me wonder if there was a platform to showcase a group of basketry artists to the world using different techniques and materials. So thank you to Brooke Munro, Cass Harris, Anna Whitelaw, Nicole Robins and Helle Jorgensen for that inspiring weekend.

Kerrie Meehan for first putting the idea in my head and me laughing it off!

Shelley Husband for sharing all the info on the practical side of getting the book started.

Especially to all the women at the Basketmakers of Victoria, other basketry groups and the basketry gatherings, who shared their knowledge and in particular the ones who taught me specific techniques and shared knowledge about plant fibre.

- Lesley Hall - random weave - everyone does it differently!
- Edit Meakin - making a melon basket and all the wonderful techniques included.
- Liz Reed - making cordage.
- Dianna Pearce - twining.
- Marion Gaemers - random weave with fine fibre.
- Robyn Norris - random weave and different methods.
- Nicole Robins - your inspiring work and use of plant fibre.
- Mavis Ganambarr - introducing me to coiling and your beautiful friendship.
- Helle Jorgensen - plant information and support along the way.

For all the artists and contributors included in the book, thank you.

Thank you to friends for their support, encouragement and proof reading. To Jane Milburn for kickstarting the process. And thanks to Genevieve McLean, Karen Mueleman, Lori Kravos, Jo Braken and Pamela Woods.

To the photographers Ben Willis and Sean Paris, and additional photographer Alex Warland.

Tony Conrad - thank you for your major support and patience.

Thanks to Leah Burgess, contributing writer.

Thank you, Jane Canaway and Eily Schulz for plant editing.

Michelle Lorimer, the graphic designer of this book who held my hand all the way through! I could not have done it without her and her expertise.

RESOURCES

Craft School Oz

www.craftschooloz.com
create@craftschooloz.com

Youtube channel with numerous videos showing how to make cordage with plant fibre, fabric and starter circles for coiling

www.youtube.com/craftschooloz

Various online workshops by Craft School Oz including basketry, sculpture, textiles and natural dyeing of fabric and raffia

courses.craftschooloz.com

Further reading

Fibre Basketry - Homegrown and Handmade. The Fibre Basket Weavers of South Australia

Edited by Helen Richardson

Order through the website or look for a secondhand copy

basketrysa.wixsite.com/basketrysa/publications

Eucalyptus Dye Database

by Sally Blake

https://sallyblake.com/eucalyptus-dyes-1

Royal Botanical Gardens Kew - Plants of the World Online

An excellent rescource for plant names and descriptions.

https://powo.science.kew.org

Supplies

Australia

String Harvest

String Harvest sells ethical and sustainable natural fibres including raffia for craft supplies

www.stringharvest.com.au
Instagram @string_harvest

Raffia Connection

Raffia Connection is an online store for crafters selling raffia and various natural threads and fibres

www.theraffiaconnection.com.au
Instagram @theraffiaconnection

Brooke Munro

Dyed raffia and basket supplies

www.mrandmrsmunro.com
Instagram @mrsbrookemunro

United Kingdom

Nutscene
Supplier of coloured raffia and string
nutscene.com
Instagram @nutscene

Rush Matters
Rush merchant based in the UK
www.rushmatters.co.uk
Instagram @rushmatters

United States and Canada

Joseph Stern
Natural raffia and some colours
www.jstern.com
www.jsterncanada.com

Sandra Kehoe
Dried willow cuttings and classes
Willow Basket Farm, New York
www.willowbrookbasketfarm.com
Instagram @sandra.kehoe.5

Royalwood Ltd
Basket weaving supplies and waxed linen thread
www.royalwoodltd.com

Basketry Groups

Australia

ACT Basketry
actbasketry.weebly.com

Basketry NSW
www.facebook.com/basketryNSW

Basketmakers of Tasmania
www.facebook.com/BasketmakersOfTasmania/

Basketmakers of Victoria
www.basketmakersofvictoria.com.au

SA Basketry Group
www.facebook.com/BasketrySA

Queensland - Townsville
www.facebook.com/FibresFabricsTownsville

United Kingdom

Basketmakers Association UK
basketmakersassociation.org.uk

Scottish Basketmakers circle
www.scottishbasketmakerscircle.org

United States

National Basketry Organisation US
www.nationalbasketry.org

FIND ARTISTS AND CONTRIBUTORS

Anne Jillet
Instagram @ellisroadarts_
www.ellisroadfibreart.com
annejillett@gmail.com

Anna Whitelaw
Instagram @poa_and_pod

Brooke Munro
Instagram @mrsbrookemunro
www.mrandmrsmunro.com

Carolyn Cardinet
Instagram @carolyncardinet

Cass Harris
Instagram @string_harvest
www.stringharvest.com.au

Catriona McLean
@catriona.mclean

Delissa Waker
Instagram @delissawalkerartist
delissawalker90@gmail.com

Fleur Brett
Instagram @fleur_brett
www.fleurbrett.com
fleur_brett@yahoo.com.au

Helle Jorgensen
Instagram @hellejorgensenart
hellejorgensen.com

Jess Leitmanis
Instagram @jessleitmanis
www.jessicaleitmanis.com

Justine Wellman
Instagram @justinewellman
justine.wellman@wellco.net.au

Kate Dick
@thequiethedonist
www.katedick-sculpture.com

Kylie Caldwell
Instagram @kyliecaldwell.art
admin@kyliecaldwell.com

Leah Burgess
leah@craftschooloz.com

Marion Gaemers
Instagram @mgbasketry
mariongaemers3@gmail.com

Mavis Ganambarr
artcentre.manager@marthakal.com

Nicole Robins
*Instagram @nicolerobins_*
nicolerobins.com
nic@nicolerobins.com

Paula de Prado
www.pauladoprado.net

Robyn Norris
Instagram @robyns_baskets

Sally Blake
Instagram @sallyblakeartist
www.sallyblake.com

Zora Verona
Instagram @zoraverona
www.yava.org.au/zoraverona
florafaunaforager@gmail.com

INDEX

African Flag, 97
Agapanthus, 70
Agave, 51, 52, 71, 73, 96, 140
Agave attenuata, 51, 52, 96, 140
Allocasuarina, 97
Anigozanthos sp., 93
animal hair, 15, 27, 28, 57, 64, 65
Anne Jillett, 9, 10
Arum Lily, 71, 89
Arundo donax, 35

banana fibre, 27, 73, 76, 77, 128, 147
Banana plant, 77
Baumea rubiginosa, 26
bilums, 11, 12
blanket stitch, 36, 130
Boston Ivy, 85
braiding, 125, 128, 129
Bromeliad, 51
Buckie Rush, 38
Bugle Lily , 86
Bulrush, 93, 147

Cabbage tree, 90
cable, 22, 23, 24, 111, 154,
cane, 21, 23, 24, 25
Carex morrowii, 35
Carolyn Cardinet, 106, 184
Cass Harris, 181, 184
Casuarina, 97
Cat's Claw Creeper, 26
Catriona McLean, 137, 184
Cattail, 93
Chasmanthe floribunda, 97
Clematis, 85
coiling, 16, 22, 27, 36, 40, 55, 64, 74, 78, 82, 87, 88, 89, 91, 93, 95, 96, 98, 103, 114, 125, 130, 136, 137, 177, 181
copper wire, 58, 59, 61
Coral Pea, 85
cordage, 11, 35, 74, 86, 88, 89, 90, 91, 92, 95, 96, 103, 106, 114, 121, 125, 126, 128, 140, 148, 162, 181, 182
Cordyline, 34, 35, 51, 68, 71, 90, 91, 140, 142,
corn, 94
creepers, 70, 84

crochet, 16, 26, 55, 57, 103, 130, 164,
  hook, 124
Cumbungi, 26, 93

Daffodil, 70, 71, 73, 91, 126, 140
Daylily, 68, 70, 71, 73, 86, 126, 140
dilly bag, 18
Doryanthes excelsa, 35, 95
Dracaena draco, 51, 52, 71, 88, 128
Dracaena marginata, 51, 52, 71, 88
Dragon tree, 88
driftwood, 10, 13, 28

Eleocharis, 35, 98
eucalyptus, 59, 60, 63, 142, 159, 182

First Nation People, 3, 31, 52, 148
fishing line, 30, 32, 33, 105, 112

ghost nets, 45, 105
god's eye, 162
grapevine, 84, 85, 161, 164
guppy catcher, 18
Gymea Lily, 35, 51, 95

Harakeke, 89
Hemerocallis sp., 86
hemp, 27, 28, 59 , 61, 106
Honeysuckle, 84, 85

inflorescence, 27, 39, 40, 51, 68, 71, 79, 80, 81, 82, 83, 140
Iris, 51, 71, 92, 126
Ivy, 84, 85, 164, 186

Jacaranda, 52, 71, 96, 140, 147
Jasmine, 85
Jonquil, 91
Juncus usitatus, 28

kakan baskets, 18, 19, 21
Kangaroo Paw, 93
Kiwi, 85
Kniphofia sp., 87
Kudzu, 84, 85

Lavender, 94
Lignum, 85
Lomandra, 10, 11, 13, 26, 27, 38, 40, 44, 87, 137, 154, 155
looping, 16, 27, 32, 108, 114, 123, 125, 148, 150, 151

Madagascar Dragon Tree, 88
Maize, 94
Mat-Rush, 26, 44, 87, 154
moulding, 124, 156
Musa sp., 176

Narcissus, 91
natural dyes, 59, 102, 182
New Zealand Flax, 68, 74, 75, 89, 90, 128, 131, 141, 142, 154, 155, 176

Palm tree, 18, 19, 21, 78, 100, 101
    Alexander Palm, 78
    Archontophoenix alexandrae, 78
    Archontophoenix cunninghamiana, 26, 78
    Bangalow Palm, 26, 27, 51, 78, 180
    Black Palm, 18, 19, 21
    Date Palm, 78, 82, 83
    Phoenix sp., 78, 82, 83
    Raphia taedigera, 100
Pandanas, 38, 46, 47, 49, 177
Passionfruit, 85
Philodendron, 35, 36, 52, 71, 95, 121, 128, 187
Phormium tenax, 68, 74, 75, 89, 90, 128, 131, 141, 142, 154, 155, 176
Pittosporum tenuifolium, 142
plant material
    drying, 71
    harvesting, 68, 69
    rehydrate, 73
    storing, 72
plastic, 30, 32, 64, 65, 66, 100, 106, 112, 124, 130, 131, 140, 148, 164
Ponytail Palm, 34, 35, 158

Raffia, 21, 25, 36, 38, 61, 100, 103, 130, 131, 137, 139, 140, 147, 182, 183
Raupo, 93
recycled materials, 6, 22, 104, 105, 108, 110, 111, 120, 131, 140, 176

Red Hot Poker, 68, 70, 87, 126, 128, 140, 142
Reedmace, 93
rope, 30, 31, 32, 35, 42, 45, 105, 112
rush, 26, 35, 38, 39, 40, 44, 68, 70, 87, 93, 98, 124, 142, 154

Sanseviera, 51
sheet bend knot, 148, 151
Sheoak, 36, 97
Siver Princess, 152, 153
Slender Palm Lily, 91
soft twig rush, 26
spiral stitch, 130, 131, 134, 135, 137
spokes and weavers, 84, 140, 145, 147

Tall Spike-Rush, 35, 98
textile waste, 6, 66, 104, 130
Thaumatophyllum bipinnatifidum, 95
tools, 124
Tulip, 92
Tussock Grasses, 70, 98
twine
    baling, 64, 105, 106
Typha orientalis, 26
Typha sp., 26, 64, 93

Variegated Arundo, 35
Variegated Carex, 35
Vines, 14, 68, 70, 73, 84, 140, 159, 164
Virginia Creeper, 85
Virginia Kaiser, 15

Watsonia, 35, 86, 97, 140
waxed linen thread, 35, 36, 106, 1058, 124, 131, 164, 183
weaving
    random, 16, 27, 64, 78, 157, 159, 161
    twining, 27, 140, 141
    under and over, 144, 145
Wilma Walker, 18
Wisteria, 85
Wonga Wonga vine, 85

Yucca, 51, 69, 90, 128

Zantedeschia aethiopica, 89
Zea mays, 94

www.ingramcontent.com/pod-product-compliance
Lightning Source LLC
Chambersburg PA
CBHW061403160426
42811CB00100B/1454